God is anything but "lite," but for some reason we try to package and brand Him as if He were a light beer. If you're looking for boring, this isn't the book for you. But if you are fed up with fluff and want something more, buckle up for a Berteau-style adventure that will leave you satisfied.

—John Bevere
Author, speaker, and founder of Messenger
International
Colorado / Australia / United Kingdom

When you meet Glen Berteau, you sense intensity, fire, urgency, and focus. You will meet him in *Christianity Lite*. Without seeking your permission, he will challenge you in every way. Glen is not seeking agreement or approval as he asks you questions no one has asked you. You may put the book down, turn off the lights, and lay your head on the pillow—but you won't be able to sleep. Sleep aid is not included with this book. Read at your own risk—and only if you want to grow. The book is heavy even though the title says lite.

—Dr. Samuel R. Chand
Author of *Cracking Your Church's Culture Code*
www.samchand.com

If you love Glen Berteau, you will love this book. Glen's *Christianity Lite* is a no-holds-barred, hard-hitting, no-compromise wake-up call to the modern church. Glen employs his unique and refreshing view of Scripture with personal real-life illustrations to make this a worthwhile and at the same time easy read. Thought provoking, convicting, and Glen Berteau at his best!

—Denny Duron
Senior pastor, Shreveport Community Church

This book sounds the alarm of awakening! With his finger on the pulse of today's church, my dear friend and mentor Pastor Glen

Berteau has written a modern-day classic! *Christianity Lite* is sure to change the conversation from Christian self-absorption to what it means to die to self, long for intimacy with a loving and powerful God, and live a pure Christian walk! In this pointed and powerful message of awakening, the reader will be subject to not only a deep desire for spiritual renewal but also an evaluation of the status-quo modern-day Christian! This book contains a message of hope for today's Christian and sounds the alarm that we must change! The world has been waiting for this message of truth. What is the message? Less of me and more of God!

—PATRICK SCHATZLINE
EVANGELIST AND PRESIDENT, MERCY SEAT MINISTRIES

Glen Berteau is a prodigy, an effective speaker, and even more articulate as a writer. I have never known anyone else who can say something in a way that is never forgotten the way Glen does. This work regarding the "lite" version of Christianity is a heavy version of writing, uncompromising and with great conviction. You will not close the last page of this book wondering what he meant. I know him from his college football days when he was called "Boom Boom," because every time he scored, there were multiple booms of the cannon. Make no mistake. The cannon is booming today in this unfiltered, straight-to-the-point message to awaken the body of Christ.

—DAVE ROEVER
EVANGELIST, FORT WORTH, TEXAS

After building a mega-ministry and raising his family, Glen Berteau has declared it's time. You're about to read something that will set the record straight. This author will reveal the real truth. Question is, can you handle the truth? It's not "Lite."

—DR. STEVE MUNSEY
SENIOR PASTOR, FAMILY CHRISTIAN CENTER
MUNSTER, IN

Christianity
LITE

Christianity LITE

GLEN BERTEAU

PASSIO

Most CHARISMA HOUSE BOOK GROUP products are available at special quantity discounts for bulk purchase for sales promotions, premiums, fund-raising, and educational needs. For details, write Charisma House Book Group, 600 Rinehart Road, Lake Mary, Florida 32746, or telephone (407) 333-0600.

CHRISTIANITY LITE by Glen Berteau
Published by Passio
Charisma Media/Charisma House Book Group
600 Rinehart Road
Lake Mary, Florida 32746
www.charismahouse.com

Unless otherwise indicated, all Scripture quotations are taken from the Holy Bible, New Living Translation, copyright © 1996, 2004, 2007 by Tyndale House Foundation. Used by permission of Tyndale House Publishers, Inc., Carol Stream, Illinois 60188. All rights reserved.

Scripture quotations marked KJV are from the King James Version of the Bible.

Scripture quotations marked NKJV are from the New King James Version of the Bible. Copyright © 1979, 1980, 1982 by Thomas Nelson, Inc., publishers. Used by permission.

Cover design by Lisa Cox
Design Director: Bill Johnson

Names and details of the stories in this book have been changed to protect the privacy of the individuals.

Visit the author's website at www.glenberteau.com.

Library of Congress Control Number: 2012912888
International Standard Book Number: 978-1-62136-226-5
E-book ISBN: 978-1-62136-227-2

While the author has made every effort to provide accurate telephone numbers and Internet addresses at the time of publication, neither the publisher nor the author assumes any responsibility for errors or for changes that occur after publication.

First edition

13 14 15 16 17 — 9 8 7 6 5 4 3 2 1
Printed in the United States of America

*In today's culture, many people want
"More me, less God."*

*We need more than a diluted, decaffeinated
version of discipleship.*

We need the real thing.

CONTENTS

one

MORE ME, LESS GOD

*In the beginning Man created God; and
in the image of Man created he him.[1]*
—JETHRO TULL, BRITISH ROCK BAND
IN THE 1970s AND 1980s

B LESSINGS, BUT WITHOUT obedience. Comfort,
but without sacrifice. Happiness, but without
repentance.

Many church leaders today communicate pleasant, positive, inspiring messages. In fact, their services are bulging with people who want to hear these promises! Their message, though, is only half of the gospel—and half of the gospel is no gospel at all. From a distance it looks like real Christianity, but it's not. It's weak and powerless. It's attractive, but it can't accomplish God's ultimate purpose to radically transform lives. It's fun to go to church where everything is positive, but this is a "lite" version of the Christian faith. It focuses on the grand and glowing promises of blessing, but it overlooks the requirements of courage, obedience, and sacrifice.

Not long ago a pastor asked me to come to his church to preach. I flew to his city and met with him on Saturday afternoon. He told me he was using a new ministry strategy to help his church grow. Confidently he explained, "We expanded our coffee shop so it's the best in town! And our media department is knocking it out of the park every Sunday. We're edgy, current, and attractive. I'm glad you could come this weekend." He didn't say it, but I was pretty sure he assumed I'd learn a lot from being at his church.

The next morning 1 was impressed by all the bells and whistles. A video looked like it had been produced in Hollywood, and the music was loud and entertaining. When the pastor introduced me, the band played a lick from "Play That Funky Music, White Boy."

It was all balloons and cotton candy.

That morning I preached about Christ's power to free us from Satan's strongholds and secret sins. The expression on the faces of the crowd told me they hadn't heard anything like this in a long time—maybe ever. The pastor had told me not to have an altar call "because it makes people feel uncomfortable." I didn't notice a small digital clock on the pulpit that was set for thirty minutes. Near the end of my message, people were visibly moved. Then the alarm went off. The entire church could hear it! I asked the pastor, "Do you really want me to stop now?" He shook his head and motioned for me to continue. That day people sobbed tears of repentance and worshipped the wonder, grace, and holiness of Jesus.

At lunch that afternoon I asked the pastor, "Are your coffee shop and media helping you see lives changed?"

He looked down and shook his head. "No, not really."

I told him, "Pastor, I know you believe in the power of the gospel to change lives. When the transforming power of God is unleashed, direction is altered, broken marriages are mended, and people gladly sacrifice because they love God so much. Let me give you some advice: drop the latte and pursue the awesome presence of Christ."

"I guess I forgot," the pastor said weakly. "I moved away from the love and power of the gospel that saved me, and I've been promoting a show." He sighed deeply and looked into my eyes. "Pastor Glen, can you help me?"

We need more. We need the real thing.

As I read the Scriptures, I find a lot of passages that challenge me to the core. A few passages are confusing and difficult to understand. I'm not talking about those. I'm talking about the ones that are crystal clear...the ones that destroy my comfort zone.

DEATH AND LIFE

Jesus had a way with words. He was as gentle as a lamb. He welcomed outcasts as friends, touched lepers to heal them, and held children in His arms. But He also demanded utter loyalty and complete obedience— nothing else and nothing less. If we exclusively focus on His kindness and compassion, we understand only part of His character, His purpose, and His heart.

Today many Christians are convinced that Jesus Christ came to earth to make them happy and successful. In the church world we seem to gravitate to books and messages that focus on success, fulfillment, and pleasure. When they experience any kind of disappointment, they believe God has let them down. Pain isn't part of the plan! They then assume God is mean because He let them be hurt. But Jesus didn't come to make us feel better about our selfishness and sins. He came to forgive our sins, transform us, and change our hearts so we find sin detestable instead of desirable. To make that happen, something deep inside us has to die.

Here's the truth: Jesus didn't come to hurt you. He came to kill you.

Not long before He was arrested, Jesus told Philip and Andrew:

> I tell you the truth, unless a kernel of wheat is planted in the soil and dies, it remains alone. But its death will produce many new kernels— a plentiful harvest of new lives. Those who love their life in this world will lose it. Those who care nothing for their life in this world will keep it for eternity.
>
> —JOHN 12:24–25

Jesus didn't come to make our normal, selfish, sinful lives a little better. He came to radically transform life as we know it. He came to kill our sinful lives so we could experience true life. A kernel of wheat doesn't flourish until it "dies" by being planted. Jesus was referring to His own death, burial, and resurrection only a few days away, but He applied this principle to us too. If we love our sinful lives—valuing success, pleasure, and approval above all else—our spiritual vitality will wither away and die. But if our love for those counterfeits dies—if we "care nothing" for them—we'll experience the real adventure of knowing, loving, and following Christ. We'll really live! It's our choice.

> Here's the truth: Jesus didn't come to hurt you. He came to kill you.

People who aren't familiar with the biblical concept of "life through death" may assume, "Yeah, but that's just one passage. Surely that's not central to the teaching of the Bible." Actually, the principle is found throughout the Scriptures. For instance, Paul's letter to the Romans contains many references to it. He explains that continuing to sin makes no sense for anyone who is a believer:

> Since we have died to sin, how can we continue to live in it? Or have you forgotten that when we were joined with Christ Jesus in baptism, we joined him in his death? For we died and were buried with Christ by baptism. And just as Christ was raised from the dead by the glorious power of the Father, now we also may live new lives.
>
> —ROMANS 6:2–4

What does it mean to follow Jesus? It means to be "joined with" Him in death and resurrection. Jesus loved the Father with all His heart; we'll love the Father with all our hearts. Jesus obeyed the Father, even when it cost Him His life; we'll obey God even when it's inconvenient and painful. We choose righteous living and obedience—not only when we're in church on Sunday morning, but all day every day. We live for God, not for ourselves. We study God's Word, we pray, we give, we serve, and we act like disciples of Christ—not to earn points with God and twist His arm so He'll bless us, but because we've already been blessed beyond anything we can imagine!

When we trust in Jesus, we join Him in death, and His blood pays for our sins. He raises us from the dead to new life. The Christian life, then, isn't just a different set of moral laws, rigid rules, or habits to follow. It's dying to ourselves and being raised back to life in Him! Now everything is different. Nothing is the same. Things that used to be so important begin to lose their grip on our hearts. We want to know, love, serve, and honor God out of a full heart of thankfulness. Our purpose has changed, our hearts are transformed, and our loyalties are forever altered. Paul sums up the radical transformation: "But now you are free from the power of sin and have become slaves of God. Now you do those things that lead to holiness and result in eternal life. For the wages of sin is death, but the free gift of God is eternal life through Christ Jesus our Lord" (Rom. 6:22–23).

We don't just sit, soak, and sour in the pew—sitting Christians hatch hypocrites! We get up, go out, and care for people around us with love, humility, and power.

Why don't more Christians live full-on and full-out for Jesus? Because they're losing the war going on in their hearts. A war? Yes, a fierce war. If we think becoming a Christian should make life smooth and easy, we need to think again. Any perceptive person already knows about the battle between our selfish desires and our longing to honor God. Paul explained it this way: "I love God's law with all my heart. But there is another power within me that is at war with my mind. This power makes me a slave to the sin that is still within me. Oh, what a miserable person I am! Who will free me from this life that is dominated by sin and death?" (Rom. 7:22–24).

The battle is fierce, but it's not hopeless. The answer to Paul's piercing question comes immediately: "Thank God! The answer is in Jesus Christ our Lord. So you see how it is: In my mind I really want to obey God's law, but because of my sinful nature I am a slave to sin" (v. 25).

In the next chapter he applies this truth to daily life. Our identification with Christ's death isn't just a theory; it shapes our choices every moment. Our choices, though, begin in our minds. Paul explains, "Those who are dominated by the sinful nature think about sinful things, but those who are controlled by the Holy Spirit think about things that please the Spirit. So letting your sinful nature control your mind leads to death. But letting the Spirit control your mind leads to life and peace" (Rom. 8:5–6). What do we think about all day every day? If we charted the contents of our thoughts for twenty-four hours, what would they reveal about our hearts and our values? Some of us don't give God a thought all day; maybe we recite a fleeting prayer or read a short verse. This is more like a witch doctor waving his hand over a magic potion. It's quick and may look dramatic, but it doesn't do any good. We don't have to be in church all day every day to have our minds fixed on God. No matter what we're doing, we can know we're in God's presence, seek His will, and do everything to honor Him. It just takes practice...a lot of practice.

At any given moment, though, we have hard choices to make. It's a lot easier to give in to our flesh and lose the battle. It doesn't work to toy with the flesh, and we don't talk it to death. We kill it through the power of the Holy Spirit. Paul tells us, "Therefore, dear brothers and sisters, you have no obligation to do what your sinful nature urges you to do. For if you live by its dictates, you will die. But if through the power of the Spirit you put to death the deeds of your sinful nature, you will live" (Rom. 8:12–13). We're not powerless, helpless victims of our sinful natures. We have a new identity and a new power to kill our flesh and walk in newness of life. Do you want real life? It's there for the taking.

If you prefer the watered-down version of the faith, Christianity Lite, you can certainly have it, but it inevitably leads to disappointment, heartache, and emptiness because it can't provide the firm foundation of hope, forgiveness, and purpose. It's self-focused, not Christ-focused. It's shallow, not deep. It's weak, not dependent on the Spirit's power. Isaiah said it's like a bed too short to lie down on and blanket too narrow to keep us warm (Isa. 28:20). It just doesn't work!

PERCEPTIONS OF GOD

Today many people have shallow, faulty views of God. Some see Him as a fairy godmother who delights in dispensing sweet blessings and demands absolutely nothing at all. Others see Him as their divine butler who should be attentive to their every whim and meet every need (preferably before being asked). Those who grew up in a strict church environment may see God as a vigilant cop or a harsh judge who sneers at them whenever they do anything wrong. None of these misperceptions result in a full heart of love and devotion to God.

Jesus calls us His friends, but He's no ordinary friend! The disciples were notoriously slow to catch on, but even they realized Jesus was the promised Messiah who had been foretold so often in the Old Testament. John's Gospel shows how Jesus's claims were inflammatory to those who heard Him. Over and over again He repeated a term that may not mean much to us, but it meant everything to the people standing around Him. He said: "I am the bread of life." "I am the door." "I am the resurrection." "I am the light of the world." "I am the true vine." "I am the good shepherd." In fact, at one point Jesus told them, "Before Abraham was even born, I AM!" (John 8:58). The Jews had a good memory. When God revealed Himself to Moses, He identified Himself as "I AM"—the God who has always existed and always will. Jesus was claiming to be none other than Jehovah Himself!

When we read the Gospel accounts, we see many different responses to Jesus. Some, like the woman who barged into a dinner party to show her love for Jesus by anointing His feet with perfume and tears, adored Him. Some, like the disciples in the boat when Jesus calmed the storm that threatened their lives, feared Him. And some, like the Pharisees, who cared more for their position in society than Jesus's care for the poor and the outcasts, despised Him. No one, though, was ever bored by Him. That simply wasn't an option. Today the lukewarm temperature of many Christians has done something Jesus's most devout followers and fiercest enemies could never do: we've made Him look boring.

THE GOD GAME

Today many of us make the mistake of treating Christianity as a game—and when the game is over, we put it back in the closet. We play with our faith, dabble in church, and are friendly with sin. We want to impress people with how godly we are, but is Jesus impressed? Could we be putting on a show for the wrong audience?

Research by George Barna shows that in most statistical categories, participation in Christian activities is slipping in America. For instance, megachurches are growing, but overall church attendance has declined by 9 percent (from 49 to 40 percent) in the last 20 years. Similarly, Bible reading and serving as volunteers has dropped during this time (5 and 8 percent respectively). But most alarmingly, the number of people who consider themselves "unchurched" has skyrocketed by 50 percent, from 24 to 37 percent.[2]

In other aspects of our culture Christians rank at or just below the broader population in the incidence of divorce, drug use, and other family calamities. The Barna Group examined American families and discovered that divorce occurs in 33 percent of all couples. Among evangelical Christians the divorce rate is only slightly better: 26 percent. Among Catholics the figure is 28 percent. Those who identify with all Protestant churches get divorced at a higher rate than the national average: 34 percent.[3]

Barna also shows a negligible "righteousness factor" in his study of adults who consider certain behaviors "morally acceptable." See if this makes sense to you:

- Sixty percent of all adults believe cohabitation is just fine; 49 percent of born-again believers agree with them.

- Fifty-nine percent of all adults think it's perfectly acceptable to enjoy sexual fantasies; 49 percent of born-again Christians do too.

- Forty-five percent of all adults accept abortion as a means of terminating a pregnancy; 33 percent of born-again believers agree.

- Thirty-eight percent of adults think it's acceptable to view pornography; 28 percent of born-again Christians accept this view.

- Thirty-six percent of adults use profanity; 29 percent of born-again believers curse and swear.[4]

What can we conclude? The level of impact Jesus Christ's sacrifice has made on people who consider themselves "born-again believers" makes roughly a 10 percent difference in moral behavior. If the gospel is the power of God for salvation—and it is—why do we see nearly the same level of sin and the same kinds of strongholds in believers' lives as we see in the lifestyles of those who don't claim to know God at all? Is the model for our lives what we see on *Desperate Housewives*, or is it the purity and fiery love of Jesus? Surely knowing Jesus should make more of a difference.

These sad facts remind me of a Wendy's commercial from a couple of decades ago. An old lady looked at a tiny hamburger lost on a huge bun, and she asked indignantly, "Where's the beef?" We can ask the same question today. Where's the commitment? Where's the zeal? Where's the sacrifice? Where's the dedication to Christ at all costs? Today the faith of many is a huge, fluffy bun but very little meat.

Advertising is a good window on our culture. Another commercial—the one that prompted the title for this book—also aired a few years ago. The first "lite" beer was a huge hit. The ads showed two crowds shouting their favorite attributes of the brew. One yelled, "Tastes great!" The other responded, "Less filling!" Both benefits were attractive to prospective beer drinkers who didn't want to sacrifice taste when they saved a few calories. During the Super Bowl a competing beer company came out with their best ad yet. This time they claimed the beer was "more of what you want, and less of what you don't want." How attractive is that? If you ask my selfish flesh what it wants, it'll tell you it longs for applause, comfort, freedom, control, and wealth. But it doesn't want discipline, sacrifice, confession, serving, or any cost at all. It wants promises, plenty, and pleasure—not pain.

The new beer was such a big hit that many other foods adopted the strategy. Suddenly we had lite margarine, lite cheese, lite cookies, lite chocolate, decaffeinated coffee, and sugar substitutes. We even have Lite Spam!

And now we have Christianity Lite...it tastes great, but it's less filling. It feels good, but it has no power. It promises more of what we want and less of what we don't want. And people are buying it like crazy.

When advertisers promise their product has fewer

calories, they mean they've tampered with the original. They want us to think it tastes the same and looks the same, but it's fundamentally changed. It's not like it used to be. Christianity Lite is fundamentally different from the original. It says God will please our senses, but we don't have to pay the price. It promises life without any hint of death.

The modern message is seductive but shallow. Christians today don't need a seeker-sensitive message that downplays the demands Jesus spoke loudly and clearly. People don't need a "user friendly" Jesus; they need the creator and Savior of the world. They don't need a decaffeinated gospel that doesn't have the power to get them up and keep them excited. They don't need a message that winks at sin and promises freedom from guilt because "after all, we're really good people." They need the real thing.

> He loves us, and He'll also expose our selfish hearts because He loves us.

We need a Savior who pays for all our sins—the ones at the surface and the ones we hope nobody will ever see. We need a Spirit who shines His light on the deepest recesses of our hearts and won't let us deny our sins and flaws. We need a God who offends us as much as He comforts us, whose power is far greater than anything we can imagine, and who leads us into the light and through the darkness. We need a purpose that's so big and challenging that it demands the very best from us—something to live for...something to die for.

Jesus didn't come to make us happy. He came to humiliate our flesh so He could transform us and raise us to a new life. He offends our pride. He offends our habits and our lifestyle. He offends our emotions and our minds. He confronts our selfishness, arrogance, and self-pity. He doesn't coddle them. He destroys them. He's not satisfied with half-baked commitment and lukewarm zeal. He doesn't care if He embarrasses us by pointing out our faults and flaws. He was exposed in shame on the cross for all the world to see. He did it because He loves us, and He'll also expose our selfish hearts because He loves us. To many of us today Jesus is saying, "I've given everything I've got for you. I'm tired of you taking Me for granted, using Me for your selfish purposes and complaining when I don't jump through your hoops. I have some hoops I want you to jump through. They'll cost you everything, but they'll give you what your heart really longs for. I want people without spot or wrinkle." To remove wrinkles from clothes, you need a hot iron. Have you ever lay down on God's ironing board?

Today we somehow have drawn the conclusion that the Christian faith should never push, pull, or unsettle anybody. Jesus is like Xanax for everyone's troubled hearts. But that's not the way He saw Himself, and it's certainly not the way others saw Him. When John the Baptist sent messengers to ask if Jesus was really the Messiah, Jesus told the man to go back and report all the miracles He had done. Then He said, "And blessed is he who is not offended because of Me" (Matt.

11:6, NKJV). On many occasions Jesus offended the religious leaders. They didn't want to lose their power over the people. Jesus was getting too popular, and He was speaking out to show the depravity of the religious leaders' hearts. After a particularly harsh statement spoken by Jesus, the disciples told Him, "Do You know that the Pharisees were offended when they heard this saying?" (Matt. 15:12, NKJV).

Yeah, He knew. He replied, "Every plant which My heavenly Father has not planted will be uprooted. Let them alone. They are blind leaders of the blind. And if the blind leads the blind, both will fall into a ditch" (v. 13, NKJV). Jesus didn't care that He offended them. In fact, He knew that the only way to penetrate their hardened hearts was to blast through. His fierce confrontations were always motivated by love. His message always offends those who aren't living for God, those who could care less, and those rules-oriented religious Einsteins who think they have it all figured out without obeying Jesus.

There are no guarantees when we live for Christ. He may make us comfortable, or He may make us martyrs. The question is: Are we pliable in God's hands? God often uses suffering to get our attention and test our faith. Will we respond in humility or with arrogant pride? Difficulties, though, are no guarantee we'll get the picture. Every heartache, every setback, every conflict is a watershed moment: Will we cling to God and trust Him for wisdom and strength to accomplish His purposes, or will we insist on our own way? A young German Christian leader faced this watershed in his life, his family, and his country. When Adolf Hitler became chancellor of Germany in 1933, Dietrich Bonhoeffer took an unpopular stand against the führer and the Nazi party. During the war he led a resistance movement. He was arrested, facing torture and death. Even in prison he never regretted his costly stand for Christ and justice. For him no price was too high. He was willing to die for Christ and His cause. Repeatedly the guards dragged Bonhoeffer to the courtroom to answer charges. The judge demanded that he give the names of collaborators, but he refused. He calmly explained that as a Christian, he was an enemy of the Nazi regime, so they threw him back into his cell. Late in the war some friends plotted to free him, but he realized the plot endangered their lives, so he refused. Before he was executed, he wrote:

> I am sure of God's hand and guidance.... You must never doubt that I am thankful and glad to go the way which I am being led. My past life is abundantly full of God's mercy, and above all sin stands the forgiving love of the Crucified.[5]

On the day he was hanged, Bonhoeffer went to the gallows with his head held high and his heart full of gratitude to God. His strong faith and dignity impressed everyone who knew him—even the prison guards. Dietrich Bonhoeffer was the real deal.

How did Bonhoeffer's faith remain strong during

his long ordeal? He made a clear distinction between "cheap grace" and "costly grace"—the same difference I'm drawing in this book. Bonhoeffer explained, "Cheap grace is the preaching of forgiveness without requiring repentance, baptism without church discipline. Communion without confession. Cheap grace is grace without discipleship, grace without the cross, grace without Jesus Christ." In contrast, "Costly grace confronts us as a gracious call to follow Jesus; it comes as a word of forgiveness to the broken spirit and the contrite heart. It is costly because it compels a man to submit to the yoke of Christ and follow Him; it is grace because Jesus says: 'My yoke is easy and my burden is light.'"[6]

The deep, life-changing experience of costly grace made the difference in Bonhoeffer's life. It makes the difference in our lives too.

Jesus welcomed all people, but He didn't leave them the way He found them. Grace is Jesus waiting for you to have a one-on-one encounter to deal with your messed-up life. It changes, transforms, and redirects you. If you think you've encountered Jesus Christ but there's no difference in your attitude and lifestyle, you need to reexamine your understanding of saving faith. In His most famous sermon Jesus told the crowd, "You can enter God's Kingdom only through the narrow gate. The highway to hell is broad, and its gate is wide for the many who choose that way. But the gateway to life is very narrow and the road is difficult, and only a few ever find it" (Matt. 7:13–14). The grace of Christ is the narrow road, the only gate to salvation. The broad path takes many forms: Buddhism and Hinduism, performing religious rituals and gaining power in organizations as the Pharisees did and trying to earn your way to heaven by giving a lot of money to the church. Christianity Lite is another form of the broad way because it denies our desperate need to be forgiven, changed, and redirected. It leaves men and women in control of their own lives and makes Jesus their servant.

Charismatic expressions—tongues, healing, miracles, and prophecies—are wonderful, but they aren't central. If they point us to Jesus, they perform their function well, but if they only amuse us, they distract from pure devotion to Jesus Christ. Blessing, prosperity, and charismatic gifts aren't the focus of the gospel. God's purpose is to rescue us from hell and shape us into the image of His Son, Jesus, so that we become light and salt in our culture. That's when He receives glory, and that's when we're truly satisfied. If we're not changed, God can't use us to change our culture.

Jesus never altered His message to fit His audience. He wasn't wowed by the rich young ruler's vast wealth. This man could have written a check to fund the new building program, but Jesus didn't care for his money. Instead Christ pointed to the idolatry of his wealth that was keeping him far from God. And Jesus wasn't tongue-tied when He met with a Samaritan woman who had had five husbands. He looked past her sin into her broken heart and offered her living water. The angry Pharisees didn't intimidate him, and He wasn't ashamed to have a prostitute break into a formal dinner party to pour perfume on His feet. He only cared that people connected with His heart so they could be changed forever.

FEELING GOOD, FEELING BAD, FEELING RELIEVED

In our society today we seem to think we have the inalienable right to feel great about ourselves. The "self-esteem movement" has swept our school systems. "Grade inflation" is used to give almost all kids a high mark, no matter how poorly they've performed in the classroom. However, the thirst for a positive self-image isn't limited to education. We avoid honesty in our homes, friendships, and businesses because our first priority is to avoid hurting anyone's feelings...ever...in the least.

Jesus never altered His message to fit His audience.

Even a casual reading of the Bible shows us that God doesn't let us off the hook so easily. He points out our sins at every turn—not because He's a sadist who enjoys blasting us, but because blunt honesty about sin is the only way to expose our need for His forgiveness and restoration. He wants us to feel bad so we can turn to Him and feel relieved. When that happens, our motivations do a 180. Our "have tos" turn into "want tos." Instead of dragging our feet at the thought of obeying God, we want to honor Him with all our hearts in every way, all day, every day.

Our culture teaches that shame is the worst possible emotion we can feel. It's not. Apathy is. An acute sense of shame is an open door to experience God's grace, love, and purpose for our lives. In his book *Shame and Grace* pastor and author Lewis Smedes explains that the greatness of God and the vastness of His creation makes him feel small, in awe of God's majesty. But the contrast between the fiery love and righteousness of Jesus and his own dark heart produces a very different reaction: a genuine, healthy sense of shame. He explains:

> I notice that Jesus never calculates the consequences before he speaks the truth; I feel a sudden pain about my self-protecting deceits. I see that he does what is right even when doing it will get him nailed to a cross; I feel a sharp pain at what a coward I am when it is risky to do the right thing. I sense how clearly he knows God's will and how he lets no sidetracks seduce him from it; I feel heavy about how easily I lose my way. I compare his love with mine; I am ashamed of my egoism and selfishness. The contrast between the Humanity of God and the humanity of Smedes shames me. Spiritual shame, then, is the price I must pay for experiencing the friendship of... God.... However, the very pain is the onset of healing, for grace overcomes the contrast and makes me feel more worthy than if I had never felt the shame.[7]

Jesus never let people off easily. At the height of His popularity He made some of His most chilling demands. John paints the picture for us: Jesus was preaching on a hillside near the Sea of Galilee. Five thousand men were listening to Him. Counting the women and children, there were probably twenty thousand people in Jesus's church service that afternoon. After He taught for a while, the people got hungry. (Nothing new there.) Jesus took a boy's sack lunch and fed the whole crowd! There were no big screens and video cameras, but everybody knew what had happened. They were thrilled! They wanted to make Him their king, but Jesus slipped off to be alone. The disciples thought they were going to be in His cabinet when He became king. They were picking out their condos in the palace!

Jesus sent the disciples across the lake. In the middle of the night a storm threatened to sink their boat. At that moment they looked across the waves and saw Jesus walking toward them—on the water!

The next day the crowds came around the lake to the other side. They were a bit confused. They knew the disciples got there by boat, but how did Jesus get there? They began a dialogue with Jesus about their desire for more miracles, more free lunches, and a happy life. Jesus saw through their requests. He told them the only bread they really needed was Himself: the bread of life. That didn't suit them. They wanted more than spiritual answers, a relationship with God, and meaning and purpose. They wanted an easy life, prosperity, and perfect happiness.

As the argument went back and forth, Jesus told them, "Stop complaining about what I said. For no one can come to me unless the Father who sent me draws them to me, and at the last day I will raise them up" (John 6:43–44). In Christianity Lite people are in control. They think they can choose to respond to God on their terms and on their schedule. But Jesus says it's different: the Father takes the initiative, and He's in complete control. If we come to God on our terms, we think we hold all the cards and assume we can get Him to fulfill our purposes. In the lite version of the Christian faith, there's little godly shame, little holy conviction, and little humility. But when we realize salvation is a gift from God—from first to last—we realize how desperately we need God's salvation, and we humbly receive His mercy, grace, and love.

In the argument Jesus didn't budge. As the demands on Him grew, He responded with clear defiance of their selfish requests. Finally He said the most offensive thing any Jewish rabbi could utter: "I tell you the truth, unless you eat the flesh of the Son of Man and drink his blood, you cannot have eternal life within you. But anyone who eats my flesh and drinks my blood has eternal life, and I will raise that person at the last day. For my flesh is true food, and my blood is true drink" (vv. 53–55).

They thought He was advocating cannibalism...with Himself as the main course! But instinctively they knew Jesus was saying, "If you want real life, you have to consume Me—My love, My passion, My purposes...everything. It's all or nothing. Take Me or leave Me. If you're all in, you get everything that's valuable. If not, you get nothing. Your call."

One of the saddest scriptures in the New Testament is found in John 6:66: "At this point many of his disciples turned away and deserted him." Thousands who had wanted to proclaim Him king the day before when He gave them a free lunch now walked away. They were in it for comfort and happiness. Obedience and sacrifice? Not so much. After the crowds drifted away, Jesus stood with only the twelve disciples standing around Him. He asked, "And how about you? Are you leaving too? Is following Me too hard even though you've seen so many miracles?"

Peter answered for the few who remained. "Lord, to whom would we go? You have the words that give eternal life. We believe, and we know you are the Holy One of God" (vv. 68–69).

Christianity Lite would solve the problem of low attendance in a very different way. It lowers the requirements on the disciples, hoping most will come back. That wasn't Jesus's plan. He kept the demands incredibly high, even at the risk—and the reality—of people walking away.

NOT EXACTLY LIKE WE PLANNED

We often say that following Jesus is the "greatest adventure life can offer." But adventures always involve risk and danger. Safety, pleasure, and thrills may be attractive, but Disneyland isn't a real adventure unless you're five years old!

Sooner or later God's path will take us places we didn't intend to go. We can count on it. He asks us to stand up to people when it would be easier to run and hide. He requires us to forgive those who don't care that they hurt us... and intend to do it again. He leads us into glorious light and blessing, but He also leads us into times of darkness and heartache. There are no guarantees we'll understand His reasons for taking us into hard times, but we can be certain He has good reasons. That's all the assurance we'll have, but it's enough.

One of the most important lessons we'll ever learn is that God's purposes are far higher and greater than ours. Our flesh wants perfect peace, happiness, and blessing. We want it all, and we want it right now! But God's purposes focus on His glory and the souls of others. He'll move heaven and earth to get us to the right place at the right time to fulfill our God-inspired destiny. But we have to be ready.

When Jesus met Paul (then known as Saul) on the road to Damascus, the young Jewish zealot was fabulously saved. God blinded him and sent him into the city. There God told Ananias to baptize Paul. Ananias was no dummy. He'd heard Paul captured and killed Christians. That's why he was coming to Damascus in the first place! To reassure Ananias, God explained His purpose for Paul: "Go, for [Paul] is my chosen instrument to take my message to the Gentiles and to kings, as well as to the people of Israel. And I will show him how much he must suffer for my name's sake" (Acts 9:15–16).

Ananias obeyed God, baptized Paul, and watched as the new believer walked into the synagogue to preach a message about Jesus the Messiah! Everyone was stunned, but Ananias knew God had much more in store for Paul. Over the next two or three decades Paul traveled across the Roman world telling everyone who would listen about Jesus. Sometimes people believed his message and got saved, but in every city those who opposed him tried to kill him.

Paul had been on the fast track for leadership in the Jewish culture. His passion to get rid of Christians was suddenly and gloriously reversed, and he became the new faith's leading spokesman. But his impact came at a cost. When the Corinthian Christians questioned his credentials, he gave them a brief history of how much he had suffered for Christ and His cause:

> I have worked harder, been put in prison more often, been whipped times without number, and faced death again and again. Five different times the Jewish leaders gave me thirty-nine lashes. Three times I was beaten with rods. Once I was stoned. Three times I was shipwrecked. Once I spent a whole night and a day adrift at sea. I have traveled on many long journeys. I have faced danger from rivers and from robbers. I have faced danger from my own people, the Jews, as well as from the Gentiles. I have faced danger in the cities, in

the deserts, and on the seas. And I have faced danger from men who claim to be believers but are not. I have worked hard and long, enduring many sleepless nights. I have been hungry and thirsty and have often gone without food. I have shivered in the cold, without enough clothing to keep me warm.

—2 Corinthians 11:23–27

Paul had shared his faith with kings and those who were demon-possessed, rich and poor, Jews and Gentiles, those who were up-and-comers and those who were down-and-outers. He counted the cost, took the risk, and chose to be a willing, ready instrument in Jesus's hands.

After one of his travels to Greece and Turkey, Paul was arrested in Jerusalem, and the Jewish leaders tried to murder him. To keep him safe, the Romans kept him in prison for years. During this time he had audiences with the rulers of Palestine: Felix, Festus, and King Agrippa. God's prophetic word to Ananias was coming true: Paul was standing before kings to tell them about Jesus.

In the third of these hearings Festus asked Paul to speak to King Agrippa and his wife, Bernice. As usual Paul shared his testimony of faith in Christ. When he talked about Jesus rising from the dead, Festus shouted, "Paul, you are insane. Too much study has made you crazy!"

He saw his opportunity to convince the king of the truth about Jesus. He responded, "I am not insane,

Most Excellent Festus. What I am saying is the sober truth. And King Agrippa knows about these things. I speak boldly, for I am sure these events are all familiar to him, for they were not done in a corner! King Agrippa, do you believe the prophets? I know you do—"

The king interrupted Paul: "Do you think you can persuade me to become a Christian so quickly?"

Paul answered, "Whether quickly or not, I pray to God that both you and everyone here in this audience might become the same as I am, except for these chains" (Acts 26:24–29).

Agrippa realized Paul was completely innocent of the charges the Jewish leaders had leveled against him. He could have set him free that day, but Paul had appealed to Caesar—and to Caesar he would go.

From this scene in Luke's history of the early church we find two important applications. First, God's plan for Paul was far more glorious and more difficult than he ever imagined. At any point along the way—when he was beaten, lashed, stoned, tortured, hungry, tired, and ridiculed countless times—he could have said, "Hey, I didn't sign up for this! Where's the 'more of what I want and less of what I don't want'?" But Paul didn't bail out. Eventually he stood before the most powerful man on earth, Caesar, to tell him the same story about his faith in Jesus. And legend tells us the man who was faithful to the end was later beheaded on a road outside Rome.

Christianity Lite never produces what it promises. It eventually leaves us with a sour taste in our mouths and empty hearts. The only life worth living is full-out, wholehearted devotion to Jesus Christ. Can you think of one person in the New Testament who experienced miracles by diluting Jesus's message?

The second point we learn from Paul's interaction with Festus, Agrippa, and Bernice is that every person has an opportunity to respond to God's gracious invitation—but the offer may not last long. We don't know if anyone else ever talked to these three about Jesus after they heard Paul. His message that day may have been their only shot.

No one is beyond the grace of Jesus.

None of us know when our time is up. We live as if we have a blank check on the future, but we don't. Someday we'll face Jesus and answer for our lives. If we haven't trusted in Him for forgiveness, it'll be a stark, dark day. Newspaper stories each day tell about men and women, young and old, who met "tragic and untimely deaths." They may have experienced a tornado, a heart attack, a drive-by shooting, or a car wreck. It could happen to you or me today. I'm not trying to scare anyone. I'm only saying that today counts. Today is the day of salvation. We have God's guarantee for this second, but not the next one.

If you haven't put your faith in Jesus, don't wait. If you sense God's tug on your heart, don't resist Him. He loves you more than you can know, and His sacrifice on the cross covers every sin. No one is beyond the grace of Jesus. Put your hand in His, accept His forgiveness, and devote yourself to the One who is worthy of every ounce of your love and loyalty.

If you've been drinking Christianity Lite, spit it out! God is tugging on your heart, or you wouldn't be reading this book. Throw your heart wide open. Stop demanding that Jesus dance to your tune, and begin living the adventure of risk and real blessing.

To those who were listening to Him one day, Jesus asked the penetrating question: "So why do you keep calling me 'Lord, Lord!' when you don't do what I say?" (Luke 6:46). Is He asking you that question today? Do you call Him "Lord" but obey only when it's convenient? At what point do you bail out on God and His purposes? Do you expect Him to make you more successful and happy, and do you complain when you experience any disappointment? Or, like a poker player, are you *all in* with Jesus—no matter what?

The daily decision to make Jesus our priority doesn't happen by gritting our teeth and trying really hard. Yes, there are choices—sometimes very hard choices— but real faith begins at a much deeper level. Jesus told two parables to make this point. In the first one a man stumbled across a treasure that had been hidden in a field. The value of the treasure was so immense that he immediately sold everything he owned to buy the field and have the treasure. In the second story a pearl merchant found a pearl of such beauty and size that he sold everything he had to buy it. What's the message of these parables? Jesus is the treasure and the pearl. He's worth more than anything the world can offer. Both of the men in the stories realized the value of what they found was far greater than anything else they owned—in fact, more than all they owned put together! They gladly gave it all up to have the treasure and the pearl (Matt. 13:44–46). In the same way, when we see Jesus as the greatest treasure we'll ever find, we'll make dramatic choices to invest our lives to know Him, love Him, and serve Him—not grudgingly or out of guilt, but because we're thrilled to know Him and honor Him.

Christianity Lite promises we can live the way we want to live and do what we want to do. The kind of life Jesus offers is very different. He came to destroy sin, embarrass the flesh, insult the sinful nature, and transform our selfishness into humility and devotion to God. Jesus doesn't want us to insult Him by going to church week after week without genuine change. More and more churches have forgotten they exist to see people transformed. Have we torn pages out of our Bibles that call us to authentic Christianity? The one I read shows me that God is a God of second chances (and third and fourth too), but He never leaves us as we were before we met Him. Jesus gave it all on the cross, and He deserves everything I can give to Him.

In the *Pursuit of God* A. W. Tozer writes a prayer that expresses my heart—and maybe your heart too.

> O God, I have tasted Thy goodness, and it has both satisfied me and made me thirsty for more. I am painfully conscious of my need for further grace. I am ashamed of my lack of desire. O

God, the Triune God, I want to want Thee;
I long to be filled with longing; I thirst to be
made more thirsty still. Show me Thy glory, I
pray Thee, so that I may know Thee indeed.
Begin in mercy a new work of love within me.
Say to my soul, "Rise up, my love, my fair one,
and come away." Then give me grace to rise
and follow Thee up from this misty lowland
where I have wandered so long.[8]

Let's be honest: the message of this book doesn't res-
onate with everyone. Christianity Lite makes promises
that appeal to our selfish desires, but it's the wide gate
that leads to destruction. The narrow way—the way of
grace-inspired obedience—is the only way to find the
real Jesus, real life, and real meaning, hope, and love.

At the end of each chapter I've included some questions to stimulate your thinking, guide your prayers,
and propel you to take action. If you're in a class or a
group, use these for your discussions.

CONSIDER THIS...

1. How would you define and describe
   "Christianity Lite"?

2. What's so appealing about this view of
   Jesus and the Christian life? Why can't
   it deliver on its promises?

3. Do you agree or disagree with the
   statement: "Jesus didn't come to hurt

you; He came to kill you." Explain your answer.

4. What's the difference between "cheap grace" and "costly grace"?

5. What are your favorite adventure stories? What kind of risks do the heroes take?

6. Why do many people in churches today think the Christian life should be risk-free? How does this perspective affect their devotion to Jesus and their response to difficulties?

7. Read Matthew 13:44–46. Is Jesus a treasure to you? What do you gladly sacrifice to know Him, love Him, and serve Him?

8. Make Tozer's prayer your own.

two

SAVED WITHOUT POWER

*I like to picture Jesus as a figure skater. He
wears like a white outfit, and He does inter-
pretive ice dances of my life's journey.*[1]

—CAL NAUGHTON JR., IN *TALLADEGA
NIGHTS: THE LEGEND OF RICKY BOBBY*

WE LAUGH AT Cal's and Ricky's view of Jesus,
but when Christianity Lite takes the power
out of our faith, we end up with an anemic,
blurred view of Christ. Today people walk into and out
of churches and are never amazed by the supernatural
power of God. People pick up their Bibles and read
them, but when they come to scenes of God's miraculous intervention, they assume, "That was then; this is
now," or "It's just an allegory. It didn't really happen."
This anorexic version of the gospel doesn't challenge people, and it doesn't inspire them either. Jesus
becomes a good friend and an example to emulate, but
He stops being the awesome Creator and the Savior

who radically changes lives. A polished, powerless message entertains people, but it can't fill the gaping hole in their souls: it tastes great, but it's less filling.

Some people come to church only to hear great music and stirring messages about God's love. They want to learn all the promises of how God is going to make them wealthy, successful, and problem-free. And above all they want to feel good about themselves—with no requirements and no change. They certainly don't want to hear about indwelling sin, impure motives, godly sorrow, repentance, curses, strongholds, the need to care for widows and orphans, tithing, witnessing—and especially about anyone going to hell! They want the pastor to say pleasant things to numb their pain and help them forget there are consequences to every choice in life.

If they don't hear this soothing message, they leave and find a church with a more pleasant message. They tell their friends, "I need a pastor who talks about God's love, not all this righteousness and obedience stuff." I guess they didn't read much in the Gospels (or the rest of the Bible for that matter). Jesus had plenty to say about the way authentic faith radicalizes a person's heart, mind, and behavior. Obedience isn't optional equipment. It's not an after-market add-on. It's a requirement for those who claim to know Jesus Christ. Pastors who really love their people preach the whole gospel, not a watered-down, "happy talk" version. They teach and model the rigorous truth that following

Christ is, simultaneously, wonderfully inspiring and terribly threatening.

We can't obey God without experiencing His power in the depth of our souls.

The lite kind of Christianity isn't a recent phenomenon. Paul warned his protégé Timothy to watch out for it in the first century. In probably the last letter Paul penned, he told Timothy what to look for:

> You should know this, Timothy, that in the last days there will be very difficult times. For people will love only themselves and their money.... They will consider nothing sacred.... They will betray their friends, be reckless, be puffed up with pride, and love pleasure rather than God. They will act religious, but they will reject the power that could make them godly. Stay away from people like that!
>
> —2 Timothy 3:1–2, 4–5

People can be very religious without being godly. They can go to church every Sunday but reject the power that changes their lives. Why would anybody go to the trouble to attend church and even serve in different ways but deny the power of God? Because happy messages about God's love make them feel better about their pride and selfishness. To them it's a significant payoff.

The issue isn't that we *ought* to be different if we claim to know Jesus; it's that we *will* be different if our hearts have been transformed by the power of His grace.

The real gospel message doesn't validate our self-indulgence. It cuts into our hearts, shows us our desperate need for God, and challenges us to be radically transformed. It's not a pillow; it's a cross. We're identified with Christ's death, but that's not the end of the story. We're also identified with His glorious resurrection. In fact, Paul told the Ephesians that the power at work in them is the same power that raised Jesus Christ from the tomb (Eph. 1:19–20)!

> People can be very religious without being godly.

DISPLAYS OF POWER

God's awesome power is central to the Bible's message. The Greek term is *dunamis*, which means "strength" or "power." The English word *dynamite* is derived from dunamis. The term is used 272 times in the Bible, and it is implied in far more. Let me give some examples:

- The psalmist recognized warfare with Israel's adversaries couldn't be won by human strength. He wrote, "Only by your power can we push back our enemies; only in your name can we trample our foes" (Ps. 44:5). And today nice buildings, fancy programs, or big budgets don't accomplish God's purposes. Those things can help or hinder God's work depending on the hearts of those involved. Whom or what are we trusting in?

- In another psalm the writer explained, "May your ways be known throughout the earth, your saving power among people everywhere" (Ps. 67:2). The power to save people from eternal condemnation doesn't "come from within." All that's inside us is darkness, wickedness, and destruction. Jeremiah said the human heart is "deceitful" and "desperately wicked" (Jer. 17:9). It takes the power of God to rescue us and transfer us from the kingdom of darkness to the kingdom of God.

- Moses wasn't an eloquent speaker, but he trusted God's power to lead him. In the same way the psalmist understood that being a gifted orator isn't necessary to see God perform miracles in people's lives. He wrote, "I will tell everyone about your righteousness. All day long I will proclaim your saving power, though I am not skilled with words" (Ps. 71:15).

- The prophet Micah stood neck deep in Israel's wickedness, but he didn't cower in fear. He told the people, "But as for me, I am filled with power—with the Spirit of the LORD. I am filled with justice and strength to boldly declare Israel's sin and rebellion" (Mic. 3:8).

- Paul was one of the smartest people the world has ever known. He had incredible insights into theology. Before he was a believer, he was arrogant. When Christ met him, however, everything changed. He learned to trust in God's power to change lives, not his intelligence. The Greeks loved to argue about philosophy, but Paul wasn't going to be baited into those discussions. He wrote the Corinthians: "When I first came to you, dear brothers and sisters, I didn't use lofty words and impressive wisdom to tell you God's secret plan. For I decided that while I was with you I would forget everything except Jesus Christ, the one who was crucified. I came to you in weakness—timid and trembling. And my message and my preaching were very plain. Rather than using clever and persuasive speeches, I relied only on the power of the Holy Spirit. I did this so you would trust not in human wisdom but in the power of God" (1 Cor. 2:1–5).

Do we see this kind of power displayed today? Is God still at work, or has He left the building? Paul wrote the Christians in Rome, "For I am not ashamed of this Good News about Christ. It is the power of God at work, saving everyone who believes—the Jew first and also the Gentile" (Rom. 1:16). The good news was powerful then, and it still is.

Nice facilities and great technology are impressive, but they can't change a single life. Beautiful music inspires us, but alone it doesn't have the capacity to permanently transform anyone. Correct doctrine is important, but it's not enough to change lives. It takes the power of God.

The Bible is full of stories—some horrible, some wonderful, many a blend of both. Again and again we read accounts of men and women who were in desperate need. They cried out to God, and He met them in love and power. When church services go too long or messages address fine points of doctrine without making applications, people nod off or look at their watches. But when the pastor tells a story of a changed life, or even better, when someone comes to the front to tell a story of God's miraculous power, every eye is glued and every ear tuned in.

I've seen people stand up in front of a church and tell the story of being cured of cancer. Some have reported, "I've been to prayer meetings before, but this was different. This time I was desperate. I went forward for prayer. Someone laid hands on me and prayed. I don't know how to describe it, but it felt like fire filled my chest. A huge load was lifted from me. The next day I went to the doctor. When he looked at the new x-rays, he was confused. He said, 'Your cancer...it's gone. You had it last week, but I can't find it today.' Pastor, God healed me. It's the only explanation."

I've heard accounts of parents asking God to heal their children of incurable diseases, and He did. I've met with people who had been addicted to alcohol and drugs for decades, but God set them free. I've also looked into the eyes of women who were so moved by the power of God's grace that they were able to forgive the men who abused them.

I met with a woman who had been working as a prostitute for ten years. Track marks on both arms and the backs of her knees showed she was using drugs to numb her pain. She told me, "Pastor, I was repeatedly beaten and raped when I was a child—until I ran away from home when I was fifteen. I became a user, a pusher, and a prostitute. I was a throwaway. I didn't matter to anybody." A tear began to roll down her cheek. "A lady from your church came to our part of town. She saw me standing on the corner waiting for my next john. She asked if she could pray for me. I'd never been interested in God or religion before, but there was something about this lady. She smiled at me. She didn't want anything from me. She just loved me. No one had looked at me like that in a long time. Somehow she didn't see me as trash. She held out her hand. I put my hand in hers, and she began praying. I felt something like electricity coming from her into my body. I think it was love. Something I'd never felt before wrapped its arms around me and held me close. All the heartache from my childhood, all the bitterness, all the despair…all of it lifted from me when I said the name of Jesus." She grinned ear to ear, and then she continued. "Pastor, I left that old life. Today I have new friends, a job, and a purpose in life. God is using me to touch the lives of other throwaway women who've lost hope. It's all because of the saving power of Jesus…all because of Him."

These stories, these flesh-and-blood examples of the manifestation of the awesome power of God, are incredibly attractive to us. Our attention is transfixed when we hear these stories of God's life-changing strength. In many churches today people are learning spiritual doctrine, but they aren't getting the Spirit of the doctrine. In Jesus's day the Pharisees knew the Scriptures inside and out. They read about God's majesty and love, and they longed for the Messiah to come rescue Israel. Then the Messiah showed up in power and might. When they saw Jesus work miracles, they weren't satisfied. He wasn't doing it the way they expected, so they rejected Him. Jesus saw through their hypocrisy. He told them, "You search the Scriptures because you think they give you eternal life. But the Scriptures point to me! Yet you refuse to come to me to receive this life" (John 5:39–40). They knew the written Word of God in great detail, but they missed the living Word of God who was standing right in front of them. The Scriptures aren't the goal; they're the arrow that points to Jesus, "the author and perfecter of faith." (See Hebrews 12:2.)

People who value Christianity Lite can go to church

regularly, read their Bibles every day, and show up at every church-sponsored activity, but they never expect a supernatural visitation from God. I'm certainly not downplaying the value of God's inspired Word. I only want to put it in the proper perspective. I've heard it said, "If you only have the Word, you dry up. If you only have the Spirit, you blow up. But if you have both, you grow up."

Luke tells us what happened when Jesus came back from being tempted by the devil: "Then Jesus returned to Galilee, filled with the Holy Spirit's power. Reports about him spread quickly through the whole region" (Luke 4:14). Not long after He returned, He cast a demon out of a man. Those who were watching were amazed. They turned to each other and wondered, "What authority and power this man's words possess! Even evil spirits obey him, and they flee at his command!" (v. 36).

Evil spirits don't obey nice sermons, and they don't flee from good programs and beautiful buildings. They only obey the power of God.

Only a short time later, a man with leprosy came up to Jesus and begged to be healed. I wish I could have seen the tender look on Jesus's face as He reached out and touched the man's rancid flesh. The guy probably hadn't been touched in many years. Instantly his flesh became as fresh and clean as a child's. Jesus told the man not to tell anybody about the miracle. Fat chance. He told everybody who would listen! Luke tells us, "But despite Jesus' instructions, the report of his power spread even faster, and vast crowds came to hear him preach and to be healed of their diseases" (Luke 5:15).

The latest technology, building campaigns, attractive preaching, and huge church staffs can't heal incurable diseases. They're cured by the power of God.

Before Jesus rose from the earth to ascend back into heaven, He made a promise to His followers. He said, "And now I will send the Holy Spirit, just as my Father promised. But stay here in the city until the Holy Spirit comes and fills you with power from heaven" (Luke 24:49). God's power was displayed magnificently in the miracles, death, and resurrection of Christ, but He didn't leave us alone. He gave us His Spirit—and the Spirit's power—to fulfill His will on earth.

We sometimes glorify the early church and think it was pure and perfect. Have you ever read Paul's letters? The people in those churches struggled with pride, lust, greed, lying, stealing, bitterness, and envy. Sounds familiar, doesn't it? But the power of God was working, and thousands were trusting in Jesus. Soon so many people became believers that the original disciples couldn't handle the administrative load. They appointed seven men to help. One of them was a man named Stephen. Luke explained that Stephen didn't care about his new title. He was far more interested in seeing Jesus change lives. Luke tells us, "Stephen, a man full of God's grace and power, performed amazing miracles and signs among the people" (Acts 6:8).

The Corinthian church had some of the most blatant, severe problems in the first century. Corinth was notorious. It was like rolling New York, Las Vegas, and Los Angeles into one city. Paul told a man to stop having sex with his father's new wife, and he had to tell the Christians not to have sex with temple prostitutes. (Don't you think they would have figured that out?) He didn't rely, though, on his oratorical skills or his brilliant insights into theology. He could have tried to argue them into submission, but he knew there was something bigger, more impressive, and more compelling: the overwhelming power of God. He explained, "For the Kingdom of God is not just a lot of talk; it is living by God's power" (1 Cor. 4:20).

Do we need the strength of the Almighty less today because our problems are somehow less severe than those of the Corinthians and the rest of the early churches? Or have we shifted our focus—from our desperate need for the power of God to the external trappings of legitimacy? Let me ask a few more questions:

- How can people be saved without the supernatural power of God convicting them of sin and convincing them of God's forgiveness?

- Why do we keep going to church services week after week and year after year if we don't see the power of God at work to transform people?

- How can men and women come to worship, go to classes and groups, serve in the church, and continue to live in

sin—from greed to resentment to adultery
to gossip—without sensing the Spirit's
conviction and genuine sorrow? Where is
the spirit of repentance?

We can keep doing the full range of religious activities with no genuine change...if God's power isn't operative in people's lives. God isn't capricious. He doesn't send His power to those who don't want it, don't believe in it, and will misuse it. Moses was on the mountain for forty days—twice—to hear from God and see His power at work. The disciples prayed and waited for ten days and nights in Jerusalem as they waited for the Holy Spirit to descend on them. Peter languished in prison for days before God answered the prayers of the people for his angelic release. God doesn't waste His power on people who don't care about it. God manifests His power in direct proportion to our desire to see Him work miracles.

We need to follow Paul's example. To the Thessalonians he wrote, "We know, dear brothers and sisters, that God loves you and has chosen you to be his own people. For when we brought you the Good News, it was not only with words but also with power, for the Holy Spirit gave you full assurance that what we said was true" (1 Thess. 1:4–5). The "full assurance" of our salvation comes from hearing the whisper of the Spirit in our hearts and the shouts of those who have witnessed His power changing lives.

I've been in church services that had beautiful music and masterful preaching, but there was no power connected to the songs or the words. But one of the greatest compliments I've ever heard was when a man told me, "Pastor Glen, I've gone to church all my life and have never sensed God's power at work in the services. I feel it here. In fact, I can almost touch it." Praise God!

MY FIRST ENCOUNTER

Years ago when I was a rookie youth pastor in Texas, the director of a summer camp asked me to preach there. My wife, Deborah, and I were given the speaker's cabin—which only means that we didn't have to bunk with the kids. It wasn't the Waldorf Astoria or anything like that. The cabins didn't have normal roaches—they were the boot-wearing, gun-carrying Texas variety. The speaker's cabin, though, had a feature the others didn't: a window air conditioner. If you're of a certain age, you remember these contraptions. They put out a blast of cold air, but only right in front of them.

I was young and inexperienced. I had agreed to preach five messages, but I had only one message in my notebook. The first night I preached my testimony. When I was finished, I wondered what I was going to say the other four times. I went to bed wondering what God was going to do. I didn't have to wait long.

At 3:00 in the morning, someone rapped on our door. Debbie asked, "Who could that be?" I got up, rubbed my eyes, and opened the door.

Larry, the camp director, looked frantic. He blurted out, "Pastor Glen, we need you. Come quick!"

I wasn't quite ready to sprint across the grounds. I asked, "Larry, what's going on? What do you want me to do?"

With wide eyes he explained, "There's a kid out on the football field. Pastor Glen, he's demon-possessed!"

The look on my face must have told him I wanted more explanation. He told me, "He's been throwing things around the bunkhouse, cursing and growling. The kids are scared of him!" From the looks of things the kids weren't the only ones who were scared. Larry continued, "We found out his mother is a witch. If we'd known that, we wouldn't have let him come. Pastor Glen, you've got to come...now!"

I wanted to say, "This is the first night of camp! Why are you asking me to help with this? Do I look like I've cast out demons before?" I must have said something that indicated some hesitation, because Larry looked at me solemnly and said, "Pastor Glen, you *are* the camp evangelist. God has given you the power and authority to help this boy."

I put on some pants and threw on a shirt, and we started toward the football field. On the way Larry explained that four young men had been trying to hold the boy's arms and legs for the past two hours. They'd tried to pray to cast out the demons, but nothing had worked. "You've just got to help him, Pastor Glen. You're the camp evangelist!" As if I'd forgotten.

A few months before Debbie and I went to the camp,

The Exorcist came to theaters. Some of our friends were freaked out by the movie, so they slept with their lights on at night for a few weeks after they saw it. When they told me about the scenes, I didn't want to see a girl's head spin around and pea soup spew from her mouth. But now I was running to a football field to help a kid who was possessed by a demonic spirit. This was no movie! I wanted to appear to be in complete control. I wanted to look confident. After all, I had four more talks to give to these kids, so I needed to look like "Walker, Texas Demon-Ranger."

The truth is, I had no idea how to handle this situation. I'd read the Gospel narratives about Jesus casting out demons, and I'd heard stories in church about pastors and missionaries commanding demons to flee in Jesus's name. But this was different. This time it was personal. It was just an evil spirit and me.

It was easy to find the guy. In the dark a dozen flashlights were shining on a single spot on the field. When we ran up to the boy on the ground, the four people holding him down looked up at me as if to say, "Finally, Pastor Glen is here. He knows what to do." If they only knew.

The young man was growling, cursing, and straining to get free. I took a few seconds to carefully analyze the situation. I wanted to approach him the right way. Suddenly I sensed God urge me to get going: "Glen, go ahead and cast out this demon! You just showed up, but these people have been wrestling with him for two hours. They're tired. Get it done, Glen! Cast out the demon now so they can go to bed!"

This was new territory for me. I knew Jesus was far stronger than the devil, but I'd never actually had to call on God's power to overcome a real demon. This was a test. I stood over the young man and straddled him. I told the others, "When I count to three, I want you to let go of him and let him up"

What was I thinking? It was like I was a professional bull rider, and I was ready for my eight seconds of fame.

I said, "Ready? One...two...three." They let go of his arms and legs. Like a coiled spring let loose, he instantly jumped up toward me. I grabbed him by the head and hair and pulled him down to the ground again. He was fighting with all his might. I saw the devastating impact of the demonic spirit in this boy's life, and I spoke to the father of demons: "Devil, I'm sick of you! This has got to stop! You've been defeated by the cross of Calvary and the blood of Christ. Let this boy go!

The boy uttered five deep, guttural, otherworldly cries, and then he collapsed.

Everyone around me (including me) stood in stunned silence. I let go of his hair and let him lay on the ground. I tried to act cool, like I'd done this a thousand times before, but I was as shocked as they were. I assured them, "You can relax now. There won't be any more trouble from demons tonight. You can go to bed." They all looked at the boy on the ground. He was motionless. I continued, "Take him with you and put him to bed. I'll bet he's really tired."

They picked the boy up and began carrying him to their cabin. Several of them looked at me and said, "Thank you, Pastor Glen."

I nonchalantly said, "No problem." I wanted to say, "If you find any more demons, call me. I'm the ghost buster. You can count on me." But I just nodded to them as they walked away.

I started back to my cabin in the woods. Suddenly I remembered a passage in the Bible when Jesus talked about casting demons out of someone. He explained that it's like kicking them out of the house where they'd been living. They needed to find a new place to live. Now this demon needed somewhere to go. I swallowed hard. If it's mad at anybody, it's mad at me! What if it came to our cabin?

I ran back to Debbie like a scalded dog. I'm glad those people on the football field didn't see the camp evangelist running like that! I opened the door to our cabin, slammed the door shut behind me, and locked it. Debbie asked, "Glen, what happened out there? What's going on with you?"

I tried to be cool and calm. "I'll tell you about it tomorrow. Let's get some sleep."

I lay down on the bed under the roaring air conditioner, but my heart was beating so fast that I couldn't think of going to sleep. I was listening for demons on the roof or trying to open the door. (A good imagination isn't necessarily a good thing at times like that.)

All of a sudden the air conditioner began growling. Then I felt something on my legs. Something was biting me! I jumped up and yelled, "It's in the room, Debbie! The demon is after us!"

I turned on the light. Debbie asked, "Glen, what in the world?"

I quickly realized the air conditioner had frozen up. That's the reason it was making that growling sound. And when that happens, it throws out little shards of ice...which had hit my legs. No demons. No bites. Just an old air conditioner.

The night on the football field was only my first encounter with demonic forces, but it was instructive. I realized that a novice minister, who knew only that the blood of Christ has supreme power, can command a six-thousand-year-old demon to flee, and it must obey. That's spiritual power.

DELEGATED AUTHORITY

To show the disciples the kind of power they could wield, Jesus bestowed His authority to them. Matthew tells us, "Jesus called his twelve disciples together and gave them authority to cast out evil spirits and to heal every kind of disease and illness" (Matt. 10:1). The power of God is a demonstration of His presence. It's amazing that God has delegated His authority and power to people like the disciples—and like you and me. It wasn't just for the twelve disciples on that particular day.

Before He left the earth, Jesus told them, "I have been given all authority in heaven and on earth. Therefore, go and make disciples of all the nations, baptizing them in the name of the Father and the Son and the Holy Spirit. Teach these new disciples to obey all the commands I have given you. And be sure of this: I am with you always, even to the end of the age" (Matt. 28:18–20). What are "all the commands" He has given them and us? The truth of the gospel? Yes. The principles of spiritual growth? Of course. But also the authority delegated to every believer to act in Jesus's name to overcome the forces of darkness.

This concept is woven throughout the New Testament. In Paul's letter to the Ephesians he instructs us to "put on all of God's armor" so we can fight "against evil rulers and authorities of the unseen world, against mighty powers in this dark world, and against evil spirits in the heavenly places" (Eph. 6:11–12). Paul's letter wasn't written for the super-spiritual, desert monks, or television preachers. The message of delegated power is for every believer.

Our authority to exercise God's power comes from an amazing identity as God's children and ambassadors. We don't use God's power to promote ourselves, but only to honor Him. Peter described our identity in glowing terms: "You are a chosen people. You are royal priests, a holy nation, God's very own possession. As a result, you can show others the goodness of God, for he called you out of the darkness into his wonderful light" (1 Pet. 2:9). When we exercise God's power to free people from evil forces or call them into light and life in Christ, we're simply living out our family legacy as God's beloved children—the King's kids.

We have the incredible privilege of passing the legacy

of power and authority to our children and our children's children. The psalmist wrote:

> Now that I am old and gray,
>   do not abandon me, O God.
> Let me proclaim your power to this new
>   generation,
>   your mighty miracles to all who come after
>   me.
>
> —PSALM 71:18

In future generations our kids won't care about the buildings where we worshipped, and their tastes in music will change by then. But they'll be thrilled by our accounts of God's awesome power and His mighty miracles. No one ever gets tired of hearing these stories.

POWER AND HUMILITY

Learning to live by our new identity requires an understanding of God's power. Some people think that trusting in God's supernatural power means they don't have to think, plan, or consult with wise, mature people about their plans. Others are adrenaline junkies who see God's power as a fix to keep them going. And a few people try to wield God's power as leverage over others. God's power is manifested in countless ways, but always in conjunction with the full range of the fruit of the Spirit. It is shaped and expressed by love, joy, peace, patience,

> We don't use God's power to promote ourselves, but only to honor Him.

kindness, goodness, faithfulness, gentleness, and self-control. If evidence of power doesn't have those characteristics, it's a counterfeit.

God reserves displays of His power for those who give Him glory for every manifestation. They realize God is the source and channel of power and the only one who deserves praise for its effects. Humility, though, comes hard for most of us. Paul had to keep learning this lesson throughout his life. In fact, the more God used him, the more he needed fresh reminders of God's greatness and his littleness. In his second letter to the Corinthians he told them he had seen a grand vision of heaven. It was so startling that God had to give him a permanent, humbling reminder. God gave him a "thorn in the flesh." Paul asked God to take it away, but each time God said, "No." Paul explained:

> Three different times I begged the Lord to take it away. Each time he said, "My grace is all you need. My power works best in weakness." So now I am glad to boast about my weaknesses, so that the power of Christ can work through me. That's why I take pleasure in my weaknesses, and in the insults, hardships, persecutions, and troubles that I suffer for Christ. For when I am weak, then I am strong.
> —2 CORINTHIANS 12:8–10

Do you want to experience God's power? It's a package deal: God only displays his awesome power in those He has humbled. In *Fellowship of the Burning*

Heart A. W. Tozer remarked, "It is doubtful whether God can bless a man greatly until He has hurt him deeply."[2] Are you willing to pay this price for the blessing of power?

The one who held all power in His hands was the most humble of servants. Jesus Christ is the creator and sustainer of the universe. Nothing is too hard for Him. But He came as a servant, humbling Himself to the point of ultimate shame on the cross between two thieves. Augustine explained the irony this way:

> Man's maker was made man that He, Ruler of the stars, might nurse at His mother's breast; that the Bread might hunger, the Fountain thirst, the Light sleep, the Way be tired on its journey; that Truth might be accused of false witness, the Teacher be beaten with whips, the Foundation be suspended on wood; that Strength might grow weak; that the Healer might be wounded; that Life might die.[3]

Mankind had the opportunity to witness Christ's mighty power only because He humbled Himself to come among us, become one of us, and pour out His love for us in awesome strength and glory.

DISTINGUISHING MARKS

What makes the Christian faith different from other world religions? Many of the other faiths have similar teaching about moral behavior. They all have a version of the Golden Rule, and they encourage people to be honest, stop stealing, and avoid murder. But Christianity has something the others don't have: spiritual power.

I was on the island of Bali in Indonesia a few years ago. The nation of Indonesia is the world's most populous Muslim country, but the island of Bali is 93 percent Hindu. People who believe in the Hindu faith have thousands of gods, and they believe in reincarnation. They believe people who live good lives take steps forward in the long process of birth and rebirth into different species. Many of them are very nice because that's what earns them points for the future, but there's no real power. In the same way, other religions promote good behavior to twist their gods' arms so they can be blessed when they die. It's all self-effort, hard work, and manipulation of the deities. Many of the religions of the world, including New Age and Christianity Lite, have plenty of nice stories and wonderful platitudes, but they don't have supernatural power. Jesus Christ destroyed demonic forces, raised dead people to life, restored sight to the blind, healed the sick, cured diseases, dispatched warring angels, and detonated a spiritual atomic bomb in Satan's house.

We aren't saved from sin by our nice behavior. We're saved by the power of the blood of Jesus Christ.

We aren't saved to become nicer people. We're saved to become people through whom God works in supernatural power to achieve His mighty works.

We gripe and complain a lot because our lives aren't what we hoped they'd be. We don't have as much money as our friend, someone else got promoted instead of us, and our children aren't the stars on the team like some other kids. Our grumbling is ridiculous. We mess around with such trivialities when a world of authority and power is available to us. There are bigger issues in life—much bigger. There's a wider purpose for our lives—much wider. There's more power for us to experience—much more. God's power doesn't come by accident or osmosis. We have to believe it, want it, and grab it. Instead of sitting around and complaining about how bad things are, we need to tell the devil, "In the name of Jesus, get your hands off my kids! Get your hands out of my wallet! Get your hands off my marriage! Get your hands off my heart!"

Peter encourages us, "Stay alert! Watch out for your great enemy, the devil. He prowls around like a roaring lion, looking for someone to devour. Stand firm against him, and be strong in your faith. Remember that your Christian brothers and sisters all over the world are going through the same kind of suffering you are" (1 Pet. 5:8–9).

> We aren't saved from sin by our nice behavior. We're saved by the power of the blood of Jesus Christ.

Don't assume you're powerless and helpless any longer. God has entrusted His power to everyone who has trusted in His Son. If you're depressed, there's a power to give you hope. If you're addicted, there's a power to set you free. If you're sick, there's a power to heal. If you're in a strained relationship, there's a power to forgive and be reconciled. There's a power to overcome your fear, loneliness, self-pity, and sui-cidal thoughts. You may feel stuck and hopeless, but God's power is far greater than chains of sin, doubt, and disease.

Don't listen to the devil's lies any longer. Camp out in God's Word, believe His truth, and have confidence in His power. You're His...it's yours.

CONSIDER THIS...

1. Why do you think the advocates of Christianity Lite feel uncomfortable with God's power?

2. Read 2 Timothy 3:5. What are some ways people can do religious activities but totally miss out on God's power?

3. Put this statement in your own words: "If you only have the Word, you dry up. If you only have the Spirit, you blow up. But if you have both, you grow up."

4. What is the connection between our humility and God's power?

5. How have you seen God's power at work in people's lives?

6. What are some needs you see right now that require God's powerful touch?

three

SAVED WITHOUT PRAYER

*The third petition of the Lord's Prayer is repeated
daily by millions who have not the slightest intention of letting anyone's will be done but their own.*[1]
—ALDOUS HUXLEY, WRITER, HUMANIST,
AND ATHEIST

AS WE READ the Gospel accounts of the life of
Jesus, one of the most startling observations is
that He spent so much time in prayer. He was
God, wasn't He? Why did He pray so much? I don't
believe it was only because He *needed* to pray; I think
He *wanted* to pray. He wanted to spend time with the
Father, enjoying the give-and-take of love and deter-
mining direction for the future.

If the Son of God was so committed to prayer, what
does it say about our need to connect with God about
the things going on in our lives?

ESSENTIAL INGREDIENT

In Christianity Lite prayer is an afterthought. People pray before meals or some other perfunctory prayer, but there's no soul-gripping, throne-hugging desperation and delight in the presence of Almighty God. The modern version of the Christian faith offers platitudes without power, and we can't have power without laying hold of God in prayer. It's absolutely essential. John Wesley, the founder of the Methodist Church, once remarked, "God does nothing but by prayer, and everything with it."[2]

"Lite" prayer is like all the other lite products on the store shelves today. It tastes great because it doesn't require much from us, but it's less filling—it doesn't connect our hearts with the King of the universe in a deep, meaningful way. Without real prayer we can't be empowered to be the people God wants us to be and do the things He wants us to do. Lite prayer doesn't cut it.

Wherever Jesus went, the power of God blew things up. Demons ran out screaming, lame people jumped for joy, dead people got up and walked out, storms calmed down, and blind people became tour guides. But the rigid religious people didn't like all this. In fact, they were so threatened by Jesus's power that they killed Him. God's power is let loose when people pray. No prayer, no power.

Many modern people don't pray because they trust advances in technology and medicine to solve their problems. The "information revolution" has, in fact, made incredible leaps, and medical researchers have found a vast array of new drugs and treatments for almost every illness. If we're not careful, we can shift our dependence from God to our smartphones, Internet connections, and pharmaceutical companies instead of trusting in God. It's not either or. Trusting God doesn't mean we don't use modern conveniences and technology. It means we see every advance as coming from the hand of God, but we never let those things replace our core dependence on God who forgives, heals, and directs. No technology, drug, or treatment can replace God.

Prayer isn't an add-on for a committed, vibrant Christian. It never has been, and it isn't today. It's central to a rich, real relationship with God. Connecting with Him is our chief delight and our biggest fight. Near the end of Paul's encouraging and instructive letter to the Ephesians, he told them:

> Put on salvation as your helmet, and take the sword of the Spirit, which is the word of God....And pray for me, too. Ask God to give me the right words so I can boldly explain God's mysterious plan that the Good News is for Jews and Gentiles alike. I am in chains now, still preaching this message as God's ambassador. So pray that I will keep on speaking boldly for him, as I should.
>
> —Ephesians 6:17–20

To Paul, prayer was as essential as God's Word and strong faith in our fight against the world, the flesh, and the devil. We simply can't be the people God wants us to be without this vital connection. We're in a fight, and prayer is our supply line and communication link with our commander.

A MODERN SUBSTITUTE

In many churches prayer seems to be an afterthought. It certainly isn't central to the heart, message, and practice of many churches today. It's enlightening to consider this question: When is the last time prayer was highlighted in your church videos, announcements, and bulletins?

No technology, drug, or treatment can replace God.

Today many churches focus on praising God, but they have very little genuine prayer. Real prayer certainly includes praise, but it's more than praise. Praise alone is a poor substitute for concerted, heartfelt, effective prayer.

Don't get me wrong. I love music, praise, and worship. I started playing the guitar in the 1960s. Praise music has always been important to me, but a few years ago I realized it had taken center stage in American Christianity. Prayer and praise shouldn't compete against each other. We need them both. Praise reminds us of God's greatness and grace so our petitions are energized, passionate, and focused.

Our church was founded on fervent prayer, and our commitment to pray has never wavered. When we started the church, we asked God to touch people with the gospel. He did. It was called "The Miracle in Modesto." Over twenty-eight nights we had thirty-three thousand documented salvation decisions. Every night people came forward and stood shoulder to shoulder from wall to wall and down the aisles so they could say yes to Jesus. Actually, there were so many people coming forward that we couldn't get all of them to fill out cards with their contact information. I think we missed quite a few, so probably forty-five thousand got saved during those four weeks.

How did this happen? Was it the time of the year? My great speaking? The graphics, drama, and technology we used? Our marketing efforts? No, none of that. The dramatic outpouring of God's Spirit to rescue men and women from hell was the direct result of forty days of prayer and fasting.

Since then we've started many new ministries in our church. We've had staff members come and go. Many have gone to the mission field or have become pastors of churches around the country. We've had countless programs, and we've made all kinds of changes in direction for our ministry. But one thing hasn't changed: our commitment to pray. Prayer is the landing strip for God to arrive. When we pray, we prepare hearts so God can appear and work miracles. To use another metaphor, prayer builds the fireplace so the Spirit can light a bonfire.

Praise is wonderful, but it can't replace life-changing prayer. Today there are Christians—and Christian leaders—who have been saved for decades but who have never laid on the carpet for an hour to petition God to transform a life...especially theirs.

Can we be genuinely saved if we're not genuinely devoted to prayer?

PLEASANT MESSAGES OR REAL POWER

Plenty of people choose churches today with one criterion in mind: they're looking for a pastor who will tell them what they want to hear. They want pleasant messages about God's love and promises about God's blessings. They'd like to be entertained by wonderful music and inspiring stories, but they sure don't want to invest time and passion in prayer.

They aren't alone. The disciples hung out with Jesus for years. Near the end of His ministry Jesus took three of them to a mountain where He was "transfigured" into a glorified state. When they came down the mountain, the rest of His disciples were in the middle of a big problem. A dad had brought his demon-possessed son to them to ask them to cast it out. They tried over and over again, but nothing happened. When Jesus came onto the scene, He cast the demon out of the boy. The people watching—and especially the disciples who had failed so miserably—were stunned. Jesus told them, "This kind can come forth by nothing, but by prayer and fasting" (Mark 9:29, KJV). Matthew records a little more of this conversation. He remembers Jesus telling the disciples, "You don't have enough faith.... I tell you the truth, if you had faith even as small as a mustard seed, you could say to this mountain, 'Move from here to there,' and it would move. Nothing would be impossible" (Matt. 17:20–21).

It's not the size of our faith that counts—it's the size of the God we're trusting in.

In the first century "mountains" were metaphors for any insurmountable obstacle or problem. We have mountains in our lives blocking our dreams, our purposes, our marriages, our kids' future, and our health. How much faith does it take to move these mountains? Only faith the size of a mustard

> Prayer is the landing strip for God to arrive.

seed, the tiniest seed in the garden. This faith is planted in the soil of God's love and power through prayer.

Going to church doesn't move mountains. Singing praise songs doesn't move them. Giving money doesn't level them. And certainly worry doesn't bring them down to size. We can be involved in all kinds of activities in the church but still have mountains that can't be moved except by prayer and fasting. Only faith expressed in passionate, believing prayer and dedicated fasting can move the seemingly insurmountable mountains in our lives.

Maybe this is the reason some of us are so confused about our spiritual lives. We think we've done everything necessary for God to work, but we've neglected to pray and fast. Some of us have worked really hard, and we're very disappointed with the results. We've tried to cast out demons, but we forgot to pray and fast. We've read books and gone to classes to learn how to be better spouses, parents, and employees, but we haven't spent time in God's throne room.

When we get serious about investing our time and our hearts in prayer, we can expect opposition. The devil whispers in our ears, "What are you doing? Prayer is stupid. You're wasting your time." His voice speaks different messages. Some of these are:

- "You don't need God. You can figure this out by yourself."

- "God may be out there, but He doesn't really care about you."

- "Your problems are too big, and besides, you caused them yourself. Do you expect God to help you now? Forget it."

- "You've prayed before and nothing happened. Why do you think it will be different this time?"

- "Look at how many times you've sinned and failed. God isn't going to work in the life of somebody like you."

The devil's voice can cause us to doubt God's purpose and power. If we're not careful, we'll sink into despair. Through the lens of faith we know God can move mountains. Through the lens of doubt, however, they crush us. When we're discouraged, what do we do? Most of us kick into RCM: radical complaining mode. We whine and moan about how bad things are, but we don't really seek God. Oh, we may pray for five minutes in the morning before we run out the door, but we don't carve out extensive time to pray and fast. Why? Because we're "too busy." Most of us can talk for hours on the phone with someone who has no ability to fix our problems, but we find it hard to spend more than five minutes in prayer with the One who has all power in heaven and on earth. Claiming to be too busy is a lame excuse. In *Celebration of Discipline* Richard Foster identifies the source of busyness on our spiritual lives: "In contemporary society our Adversary majors in three things: noise, hurry and crowds. If he can keep us engaged in 'muchness' and 'manyness,' he will rest satisfied." And then he relates the observation of the famous psychiatrist Carl Jung: "Hurry is not *of* the Devil; it is the Devil."[3] Remember: God leads; Satan pushes.

I talk to Christians in business, and they often say their success comes from a new sales technique or new product. I talk to parents, and some tell me their kids are excelling because they're in the right school or on the best athletic teams. I talk to pastors who are in the church growth movement, and they promote a vast array of new technologies, strategies, and programs. When people ask me why our church is thriving, I tell them it's because God answers prayer. Of all the ingredients needed to experience supernatural blessings and to break strongholds, prayer is essential.

In our culture we expect perfect peace and affluence.

We think it's our right to be completely comfortable, wealthy, and good-looking. The truth is that there has never been a more prosperous society. We are—by far—the richest and most comfortable society the world has ever known. But one thing drives us to our knees like nothing else: desperation. When everything else has failed, when all the other resources have dried up, when we have nowhere else to go for help, we finally turn our faces to God...or to the floor...because we finally know only He can meet our needs.

At a critical point in Israel's history King Hezekiah became deathly ill. God sent Isaiah to give him some bad news: "This is what the LORD says: 'Set your affairs in order, for you are going to die. You will not recover from this illness'" (Isa. 38:1).

The king realized he had only one recourse: to ask God to spare his life. He turned his face to the wall and prayed, "Remember, O LORD, how I have always been faithful to you and have served you single-mindedly, always doing what pleases you" (v. 3). He wept bitter, desperate tears.

The Lord heard the king's plea. The Lord told Isaiah, "Go back to Hezekiah and tell him, 'This is what the LORD, the God of your ancestor David, says: I have heard your prayer and seen your tears. I will add fifteen years to your life, and I will rescue you and this city from the king of Assyria. Yes, I will defend this city'" (vv. 5–6).

You can move forward without friends. You can move forward without money. You can move forward without a job. You can move forward without health. But you can't move forward without prayer.

Sometimes God answers quickly, but often He wants us to persist in prayer. We prefer microwave miracles; He wants slow-simmered maturity. God often delays answering our prayers for a number of reasons: He uses the time to prepare our hearts, to test our motives, to alter the situation, or change a person's heart. But there might be another cause for the delay. An ongoing battle exists beyond time and space. The prophet Daniel prayed for three weeks for God to give him an answer to his prayer. Finally he had a vision. An angel appeared to him and said:

> Don't be afraid, Daniel. Since the first day you began to pray for understanding and to humble yourself before your God, your request has been heard in heaven. I have come in answer to your prayer. But for twenty-one days the spirit prince of the kingdom of Persia blocked my way. Then Michael, one of the archangels, came to help me, and I left him there with the spirit prince of the kingdom of Persia. Now I am here to explain what will happen to your people in the future, for this vision concerns a time yet to come.
>
> —DANIEL 10:12–14

A demonic "prince" had been blocking the answer to Daniel's prayer. It took an archangel's power to free the angel so he could come to Daniel and deliver God's message. We see only a zillionth of what's going on in the heavenly realms. We may think we have it all figured out, but we don't. However, we can trust that God will ultimately overcome evil and have His way.

As we pray, delays aren't the end of the world. We just need to pay attention, stay focused, and keep our hearts fixed on Jesus. Sooner or later the answer will come.

MOTIVATIONS TO PRAY

If prayer is so important, so powerful, and so inspiring, why don't we pray more than we do? It's interesting that every person I've ever met says he or she needs to pray more. Those who pray little feel guilty that they don't pray very much, and those who pray a lot realize they've only begun to tap into the vast resources of God's love and power. We need to understand some important motivations to pray.

Prayer empties the heart of its worries.

New technologies promised to make our lives simpler, easier, and less troubled, but today our lives are more complex, full of things that need to be fixed, and clouded by worries over the added activities and responsibilities. The levels of stress are exceptionally high, even among those who have plenty of money and are the envy of their friends.

Jesus told a story about four kinds of soil: the hard path where people walk, shallow soil with rock underneath, soil choked with weeds, and fertile soil. He described the third kind, the soil choked with weeds, this way: "The seed that fell among the thorns represents those who hear God's word, but all too quickly the message is crowded out by the worries of this life and the lure of wealth, so no fruit is produced" (Matt. 13:22).

That's the picture of many people in churches today. Christianity Lite can't provide the power to overcome these worries because it doesn't connect us with the living, awesome God. To keep all the cares of the world from overwhelming our hearts, we need the supernatural touch of God's wisdom, love, and strength. When we have His perspective, we can put things in their proper place. Jesus said that the pure in heart will see God (Matt. 5:8). We want our hearts to be pure so we can sense His nearness every day. They can only be pure if the weeds of worry are pulled out and thrown aside.

Some people are overwhelmed by their concerns. They're so discouraged they don't want to go to church. They neglect the one place where their spirits can be refreshed and their faith strengthened. And if they go to a worship service, their minds drift back to all the worries and heartaches that have blanketed their hearts all week.

When we pray, we take all those things to the foot of the cross. There *things* change. There *we* change.

How often do we need to empty our hearts of worries? Jesus told us to pray, "Give us this day our daily bread" (Matt. 6:11, NKJV). We can eat just once a week and survive, but we can't pray once a week and be spiritually strong. Peter instructed us, "Give all your worries and cares to God, for he cares about you" (1 Pet. 5:7). He cares about us all day every day, so we can pray at every moment no matter what we're doing.

Hannah was weighed down with heartache because she couldn't have a child. She went to the temple and poured out her heart. As she prayed, she was so enraptured in seeking God that people thought she was drunk. She wasn't drunk. She was more in tune with God than ever before. She was desperate to transfer her cares to the one who could do something about them. Nine months later she had a son named Samuel.

Over and over in the Bible we read about people who didn't wallow in self-pity. Instead they took their worries to God, and He answered them. Abraham, Jacob, Jonah, Elijah, David, and the others recognized they couldn't solve their own problems. They needed God to intervene. David remembered:

> I prayed to the LORD, and he answered me.
>   He freed me from all my fears.
> Those who look to him for help will be
>   radiant with joy;
>   no shadow of shame will darken their faces.
> In my desperation I prayed, and the LORD
>   listened;
> he saved me from all my troubles.
>   —PSALM 34:4–6

Do you have troubles, cares, and worries? Of course you do. You're a fallen human being living in a fallen, evil world. We all have them. Don't forget to cast your cares on God's broad shoulders. He can handle them.

Prayer acknowledges that the answer is beyond our ability.

When we look into the abyss of our struggles, we first frantically try to control the people and the situations. Sooner or later we realize all our efforts are useless. The problem is much bigger than anything we can handle. When we pray, we bow in humble admission that we're powerless. Pride insists that we know it all and can make it work out, but humility acknowledges there's a far greater power and far higher wisdom than our own.

Shrewd people in every field of life instinctively grasp their need for higher wisdom. In business the best leaders realize they don't have to know everything about every product and process, so they surround themselves with really bright people. Parents—especially parents of teenagers—quickly realize they don't have all the answers. Dumb parents keep plodding along in their ignorance and repeat tons of mistakes, but shrewd parents find others who have been down this road and can teach them how to navigate the difficult waters. As we chart the path for our lives, we don't have to know everything, but we need to be closely connected to the one who knows all the answers.

I don't need a sure-fire formula for success, and I don't need guarantees for each step along the way. But I need a relationship with someone who can lead me as I take the next step. I go to God—my loving

Father and the creator of the universe—and trust Him to guide me, provide for me, and encourage me along the way.

Prayer shows me how small and needy I really am. It's humbling, but it also reminds me that I'm connected to the greatest power source the world has ever known.

Decisions and directions come from prayer.

We live in an instant society. We expect instant answers to every question and immediate solutions to every problem. We hate to wait, but in God's kingdom waiting is an essential ingredient in prayer. Some of us wonder why God doesn't answer us quickly when we pray. Didn't He promise to answer? Surely He's quicker than the Internet! Here's a newsflash: spiritual life is a little different from online connections. Here's another important thing to remember: the teacher doesn't talk when the students are taking a test. Waiting is one of the tests of our faith—not to trip us up, but to show us what we know and don't know. While we're waiting, God is often silent. He's watching to see if we'll bail out or if we'll continue to trust, if we'll shake our fists at Him or if we'll stay on our knees. Decisions and directions, especially important ones, seldom come quickly. Be patient and persistent to seek God's face.

When we pray, we bow in humble admission that we're powerless.

But monumental decisions aren't the only thing worthy of our prayers. Paul said, "Pray about everything"

(Phil. 4:6). Everything? Yes, everything. We can pray about our businesses, our next deal, the promotion, our children's teachers, buying a new television, painting the house, how to handle an offense from a friend, which book of the Bible to study next, our tempers, how we manage our time, and every other thing under the sun. Nothing is too big or too small for God's attention.

When we pray, we won't necessarily have pleasant feelings and calm assurance. Sometimes God's leading threatens us to the core. We may not like the answer, but God will give it. On the night Jesus was arrested, He went to the Mount of Olives to pray. He faced the greatest spiritual, emotional, and physical pain anyone would ever endure. He wanted to run. He prayed, "Father, if you are willing, please take this cup of suffering away from me." But He didn't stop there. He was willing to obey no matter what the answer would be. He poured out His heart to the Father, "Yet I want your will to be done, not mine" (Luke 22:42). His heart was crushed by the prospect of bearing the sins of the world—including yours and mine. Luke tells us what happened: "Then an angel from heaven appeared and strengthened him. He prayed more fervently, and he was in such agony of spirit that his sweat fell to the ground like great drops of blood" (vv. 43–44). God's answers aren't always pleasant, but they are always part of His grand design to reach the world with the message of His grace. We need to remember the bigger picture—and Jesus's example of courage—when we get an answer we don't like.

If Jesus Christ sensed a need to ask for clarity and direction when He prayed in the garden, how much more do we need to seek guidance from God? The Lord told us to pray that God's eternal purposes would be accomplished on earth in space and time. Prayer is the umbilical cord between heaven and earth. When we pray, we're tapping into God's heart, God's will, and God's power here and now.

Some of us are pretty dumb. Like the disciples around Jesus, we keep misunderstanding God's purposes. (By the way, the more I understand my own heart, the more I see I'm a lot like those guys. I'm a lot more patient with them now!) Why do we think we know more than Almighty God? Why do we assume we can figure things out without His direction? At some point maybe we'll snap out of our self-assurance and pride so we realize the vast, untapped resources of God's wisdom and power available to us.

Arrogant people don't see any need to pray because they're confident they have it all figured out on their own. We could put it a different way: those who don't pray foolishly assume they don't need God's wisdom.

Prayer builds a real relationship with God.

We need to remember that prayer is a dialogue, not a monologue. Some of us don't pray much at all, but many of us go to God with our grocery list of wants and needs. After we go through the list, we get up and go on with our day. How would you like it if your spouse or child or best friend treated you that way? I wouldn't appreciate it, and you wouldn't either.

We talk about having "a relationship with God." In a relationship people connect on a heart level, they share their deepest hopes and fears, and they listen to the other person. Without this give and take, there's no relationship.

Many people pray like they're talking to some guy overseas who answers the phone when you have a problem with your credit card. (These guys always say their name is Bob or Jim or something like that.) It's true that when we become Christians, we get a hotline to God Himself. It's magnificent, but we may still treat Him as if He's an agent for the credit card company. Our prayers are all about us: our wants, our needs our desires, our pleasures...and we expect to have those problems solved right now!

When we have a problem, many of us pick up our phone to call God. We dial 1-800-C-R-Y-B-A-B-Y. We tell Him what we want, and we complain that He hasn't done everything exactly as we expected. Surely God should be able to fix our problems more efficiently! As we complain, our blood starts boiling. We remember all the times when God didn't come through. We remind Him, "You know those promises about money? I tithed, but heaven didn't open with showers of blessings. I've got bills, God. I'm sure you can see them on my desk. You're everywhere all the time, so I know You see them. Do You notice all the red ink on them? That's not good. Actually, I think it's Your fault that I'm past due on several of them. I'm not happy with the service, God. Not happy at all!" We slam the phone down and walk off.

We may call back a week or two later with a different complaint: "God, it's me again. Yeah, I've got another problem. As You remember, I've asked You for healing a bunch of times. I've gone forward to be anointed so many times that I could fry chicken in all the oil that's dripped down my face! God, here's the deal: I'm still sick. It's not supposed to be like this. I've done my part, and it's way past time for You to do Your part. How about it? Now would be a good time. If you don't do something quick..."

Some women pray like this: "Lord, do You see my husband? What a loser! He's in the living room lying on the sofa with his huge belly hanging out with a bowl of popcorn sitting on it. Is this the 'man of God' You had in mind for me? I don't think so. What are You going to do about him? You know I've prayed. I've asked You to change him. Oh, he's changed all right. He's gotten worse! Are You even listening when I pray?"

Many of us call back any number of times to see if God will finally come through and make our lives happy, healthy, and successful, but some of us eventually give up. We quit praying, quit tithing, and quit going to church.

Don't call God, dump on Him, and then hang up in anger. The analogy with the service agent overseas is painfully close to the way many of us relate to God. We think it's His job to solve our problems—and to be honest, we resent the fact that we even have to ask! If

He were really doing His job, we wouldn't have those problems in the first place!

When we pray, we need to remember who is listening. We have a real relationship, but we're not equals. We need a huge dose of respect for our heavenly Father. He dwells "in unapproachable light" (1 Tim. 6:16, NKJV). He knows the end from the beginning, and He knows our thoughts and hidden intentions far better than we do. We often treat Him like a butler or a fairy god-mother, but He's nothing of the kind. When Isaiah had a vision of the glory of God, he became terribly aware of his sinfulness and his need for forgiveness. When Peter saw Jesus bring in a miraculous catch of fish, he bowed before Him and begged, "Oh, Lord, please leave me—I'm too much of a sinner to be around you" (Luke 5:8). God isn't obligated to fulfill our purposes. Instead our job is to align our hearts with His divine will. He graciously guides us, but we have to remember that His purposes are always—always—far bigger and more complicated than we can imagine. God told Isaiah:

> "My thoughts are nothing like your thoughts,"
>   says the Lord.
>   "And my ways are far beyond anything you
>   could imagine.
> For just as the heavens are higher than the
>   earth,
>   so my ways are higher than your ways
>   and my thoughts higher than your thoughts."
>   —Isaiah 55:8–9

At the climax of Paul's description of God's sovereign and gracious rule in his letter to the Christians in Rome, he explodes in praise and wonder about God's majesty and wisdom:

> Oh, how great are God's riches and wisdom and knowledge! How impossible it is for us to understand his decisions and his ways!

> For who can know the LORD's thoughts?
> Who knows enough to give him advice?
> And who has given him so much
> that he needs to pay it back?

> For everything comes from him and exists by his power and is intended for his glory. All glory to him forever! Amen.
> —ROMANS 11:33–36

Do these perceptions of God's greatness and grace make a difference in our prayers? You bet they do! When we think deeply about God's unsearchable wisdom, power, and love, we realize we can trust Him—even in our darkest times and our deepest struggles. We won't treat Him like the customer service rep who seems slow to fix our problem. We pour out our hearts to Him, but we never demand that He jump through our hoops. We stop blaming Him for all our heartaches. We no longer expect God to rescue us *out of* our problems; instead we ask Him for strength and wisdom to endure *through* them. We learn that times of delay and difficulty are part of His plan to drive us deeper into an experience of His heart. We plead with Him, but without demands. We enjoy praising Him with no strings attached. We tell Him everything on our hearts, but we also take time to listen so His Spirit can remind us of truth from His Word and whisper to our hearts.

Jesus is our friend, but our friend is the King.

Prayer changes us.

Prayer doesn't twist God's arm to get Him to do what we want Him to do. It puts us in touch with His heart and His purposes so we can conform, we can change, and we can want what He wants. We need to quit trying to change God. He's perfect. How can we improve on that? When we pray, do we expect to change God? I hope not! Prayer changes us. It changes our perspective, our attitude, our understanding, and our ability to handle the situation. When we pray, we open our hearts and minds to God. We ask Him to fill us with His will, His desires, and His power. We recognize that He's the Lord; we're not. He has all wisdom; we don't. He can accomplish all things according to the counsel of His will; we can only follow and obey.

We may assume that the first thing God needs to do is meet our needs, but that's usually wrong. The first thing God needs to accomplish is to transform our hearts so our desires align with His. Then we stop demanding and complaining, and we become partners (junior partners, but still partners) in the greatest enterprise the world has ever known—rescuing people from hell and restoring them to God.

After King Solomon built the temple in Jerusalem, God appeared to him one night and told him, "Then if my people who are called by my name will humble themselves and pray and seek my face and turn from their wicked ways, I will hear from heaven and will forgive their sins and restore their land" (2 Chron. 7:14). If we humble ourselves before God to pray, He'll move that mountain in our lives. He'll move the mountain of our child's rebellion, our depression, our spouse's addiction, our debt, and every other problem. He may not move it immediately, and He may change us first, but we can be assured that God's promises are sure. God will work in His power, in His way, and in His timing. If we'll pray, God will move mountains.

Prayer gives us an accurate picture of our problem and our God. We need to lie at the feet of God; gaze into His beauty, grace, and greatness; and trust Him to do what only He can do.

COME BOLDLY

The writer to the Hebrews encourages us, "So let us come boldly to the throne of our gracious God. There we will receive his mercy, and we will find grace to help us when we need it most" (Heb. 4:16). In Christianity Lite people either demand God to fix their problems immediately, or they don't see any need to pray at all. Boldness and humility, though, are much different from arrogance and discouragement. We have a real relationship with the God of the universe. It is our highest privilege to be called His sons and daughters, but we need to remember that it took the blood of God's Son to pay the price for us to sit at His table and bow before His throne.

John Newton was the captain of a slave ship, but he was gloriously saved. We know him best as the author of "Amazing Grace," but Newton wrote other great songs. He realized that if God is our High King, there's no request too great to lay at His feet. He encourages us to be bold:

> Thou art coming to a King,
> Large petitions with thee bring,
> For His grace and power are such,
> None can ever ask too much;
> None can ever ask too much.[4]

God isn't our butler, waiter, or fairy godmother. He is the great King above all kings. He spoke, and the galaxies were flung into space. And we are His beloved, adopted sons and daughters. We come before the throne with boldness and confidence because we trust in His awesome love and power.

CONSIDER THIS...

1. What are some differences between Christianity Lite prayers and authentic, throne-hugging prayer?

2. What's the proper role of praise in church? When might it become a substitute for prayer? How can it stimulate and deepen our prayers?

3. What are some excuses you've heard (or you've used) to avoid praying?

4. How do people interpret delays when they pray? Why is it important to see delays as times of testing and preparation?

5. How does prayer empty the heart of worries?

6. How does God use prayer to give us direction and decisions?

7. How does remembering God's majesty and grace affect our prayers?

8. What is a mountain you're asking God to move right now?

four

SAVED WITHOUT COST

*If you want to follow Jesus, you had
better look good on wood.*

—ANONYMOUS

S*AVING PRIVATE RYAN* is the fictional story of
finding and rescuing a single soldier shortly after
the Allied invasion at Normandy in World War
II. In Washington General George C. Marshall learns
that three brothers have been killed in combat in battles around the world. Their mother will get all three
dreaded telegrams on the same day. A fourth brother,
Private James Frances Ryan, is part of the 101st Airborne Division that jumped behind German lines early
on D-Day, but he's missing in action. Marshall gives
the command to find Private Ryan and send him home
to his mother. At Normandy Captain John Miller
picks seven men for the mission. They search the edges
of the broad battlefield for the young man, and several
in the squad are killed. Finally they find Ryan in the

French village of Ramelle. Before they can take him away, the Germans attack. Ryan refuses to leave his outmanned, outgunned Airborne comrades, so Miller and the remaining members of his squad stay to help defend the town.

The Germans arrive with tanks, cannon, and heavy machine guns, but the Americans knock out two tanks and inflict heavy casualties. The German firepower is too great, however, and most of the Americans are killed. Before his final, desperate act of blowing up the bridge, Miller is mortally wounded. Ryan rushes to his side, and the captain whispers, "James, earn this. Earn it." Then Miller dies. At that moment American fighters appear and blast the German tanks and infantry.

The movie ends as it began, with an aging Ryan looking at Captain Miller's headstone in the cemetery at Normandy. He has tried to live his life in a way that honors the sacrifice Captain Miller and his squad made years before when they died to save his life. At Ramelle, Miller had counted the cost and gave his life to rescue a single soldier. Ryan had counted the cost the captain and the others had paid, and it changed his life.

GET REAL

We live in an age of softies and quitters. We want to eat chocolate cake without gaining weight. We expect to have lean bodies without the effort and discipline of exercise. We want new cars and houses without thinking about the ravages of debt. We demand easy love, sex, money, school, marriage, parenting, and everything else imaginable. We're sure life should be fun. When we have to put out some effort and exercise a modest amount of discipline, we soon quit because "it's just too hard."

Christianity Lite follows the same lines. Many people who claim to be believers are absolutely sure God exists to make their lives pleasant. They love promises of blessing, and they don't want to hear anything about struggle, pruning, testing, and the process of growth.

Jesus was under no such illusions. He was well aware that following Him required great cost. Yes, there are wonderful blessings, but always at a sacrifice—first to Himself, but also for us. He didn't sugarcoat the price we have to pay. When we read the Gospels, we find that at the height of His popularity, Jesus sifted out those who weren't willing to pay the price of loyalty and obedience. Many church leaders today wouldn't dare raise the bar when their churches are full, but Jesus raised it to heaven. He was willing for people to walk away. He was perfectly happy to have a few who would stay, as long as they had realistic expectations of what it meant to follow Him. Luke tells us:

> A large crowd was following Jesus. He turned around and said to them, "If you want to be my disciple, you must hate everyone else by comparison—your father and mother, wife and children, brothers and sisters—yes, even your own life. Otherwise, you cannot be my disciple.

And if you do not carry your own cross and
follow me, you cannot be my disciple."
                                    —LUKE 14:25–27

Jesus doesn't force anyone to follow Him. He makes
a proposition: if we *want* to follow, we have to *pay* the
price. We can choose to walk away, or we can choose
to take His hand. It's entirely up to us. But we should
be under no illusions about what it means to say yes to
Jesus. In the first-century culture family was everything.
In our country we have a society of "rugged individu-
alism," and we value the rights of every person. Their
culture was different. People had no identity apart from
their families and their close-knit communities. This
fact makes Jesus's words even more poignant. To follow
Him, we have to "hate" everyone else. Wait a minute!
That can't be right. Didn't Jesus say to love our neighbors? Who is more of a neighbor than our parents, sib-
lings, and extended family?

The concept of "hating" people isn't that we want to
kill them. It's the idea of preference. When I choose
broccoli over cauliflower at the cafeteria, I'm making
a preference. My choice shows my "love" for broccoli and my "hate" of cauliflower. That's the point in
Jesus's statement. When we follow Him, we're saying
we prefer Him, we honor Him, and we're loyal to
Him above everything and everyone—even the human
beings who are closest to us. When there's a choice to
be made, we choose Jesus instead of our spouse, kids,
mom, dad, brother, or sister. In fact, we choose Jesus's
honor, glory, and fame over our own comfort, wealth,

pleasure, and reputation. That's what it means to call Him "Lord." Either Jesus is our Master, or He's not. If He is, we obey Him even when it's uncomfortable or costly. If He's not, we continue to invest our resources in selfish gain and pleasures, and we try to use God as a tool to get what we want.

At this point in Luke's Gospel Jesus had been doing all kinds of miracles. People loved that! But entertaining people and building a large crowd weren't Jesus's goals. He wanted to find men and women who would love Him supremely and follow Him completely. He said we can't be His disciples—His true, loyal, committed, obedient followers—unless we put Him first in our lives. Jesus doesn't want to be added to the list of prior ities and be juggled between number seven and number thirty-two. He insists on being number one. Number two isn't acceptable, right, or reasonable.

Whenever crowds followed Jesus only for selfish pur poses, He reminded them that it's not about them at all—it's all about Him and His glory. It's the same today. If we're willing to sign on to put Him first, we'll have countless blessings thrown in. But if we focus pri marily on the blessings, we'll get neither Jesus nor the blessings. There are a lot of people in churches today who come every Sunday, but only for the blessings. They don't really love Jesus more than anyone or any thing else. They're consumers, not worshippers. They just want the blessings, and they're very disappointed in Him when He doesn't deliver.

To make sure those listening to Him understood,

Jesus gave them two examples. First He used a construction metaphor:

> But don't begin until you count the cost. For who would begin construction of a building without first calculating the cost to see if there is enough money to finish it? Otherwise, you might complete only the foundation before running out of money, and then everyone would laugh at you. They would say, "There's the person who started that building and couldn't afford to finish it!"
>
> —LUKE 14:28–30

This is an example many of us can understand. If we want to build a home, remodel a kitchen, or do any other major work around the house, we don't start until we've figured out how much it's going to cost. Most of us have grand ideas, but when we see the numbers, we have to adjust the plans to fit our budget. We'd be dumb to start a project before we did the financial calculations. Jesus is saying, "Don't be foolish. Don't even start following Me until you realize the cost—which is giving Me everything you've got. I'm asking you to die. That's not too much, is it?"

But Jesus wasn't finished. Foreign armies often marched through Palestine. The history of Israel was full of wars, battles, invasions, and exile. At that time the Roman army occupied Israel. Jesus used a military example that would be familiar to every person listening:

Or what king would go to war against another
king without first sitting down with his coun-
selors to discuss whether his army of 10,000
could defeat the 20,000 soldiers marching
against him? And if he can't, he will send a
delegation to discuss terms of peace while the
enemy is still far away. So you cannot become
my disciple without giving up everything you
own.

—LUKE 14:31–33

Building a house without counting the cost proves
embarrassing when we can't finish it, but going to war
without thinking it through results in blood, death,
and misery. In His military example Jesus speaks to
human pride. A king wants to look strong and confident to his own people and the enemy, but prudence
dictates a diplomatic course if he doesn't have the firepower to defeat his enemy.

So, in His teaching about preference and the two
metaphors, Jesus invites us to follow Him, but He
reminds us that we'll have to pay a hefty price:

- We have to prefer Him over our closest
  human relationships.

- We have to love Him more than our own
  comfort, pleasure, success, and reputation.

- We have to count the cost before we start
  so we are fully aware of the investment of
  heart, time, and treasure.

- Nothing can be held back. We can't be fully His unless we give up everything.

Jesus concludes His outline of the cost of discipleship with a comment about salt. He said, "Salt is good for seasoning. But if it loses its flavor, how do you make it salty again? Flavorless salt is good neither for the soil nor for the manure pile. It is thrown away. Anyone with ears to hear should listen and understand!" (Luke 14:34–35). In that day people didn't go to the grocery store to buy nice containers of pure salt. Most of the salt they used came from the Dead Sea, and it originally contained contaminating minerals such as gypsum. If the people mining and selling didn't purify it, the salt would taste bad and be completely useless. In the same way we begin with considerable impurities (greed, lust, lying, selfishness, and all kinds of other bad attitudes and behaviors). Jesus is a realist. He knows we're deeply flawed and need to go through a process to purify our motives and habits. This process isn't optional. If we don't give ourselves to the process of purification (also called sanctification or spiritual growth), we become less than worthless!

In a nation of quitters this message sounds terribly odd and offensive. If Jesus invited us to run with Him in a marathon, we'd have similar choices to make. We might quickly agree to run the race, but most of us would drop out after the first mile or two. It would be embarrassing. But if we count the cost, we might train for months before we hit the streets. The time of training prepares us for the race set before us.

Today many people start school, but they drop out when it gets too hard. They start diets, but they grab a whole bag of chips and eat a huge bowl of ice cream after only two days. They start a marriage, but they walk away when it's not pleasant anymore. They start raising children, but they emotionally back away when the kids are hard to handle. They start a career, but they lose interest when the pay doesn't seem to match the responsibilities. They start walking with Jesus, but in times of testing they drift away and become luke-warm hypocrites.

Paul compared the Christian life to an Olympic event. We are all, he explained, spiritual athletes competing in the greatest race of all. He told the Corinthians:

> All athletes are disciplined in their training. They do it to win a prize that will fade away, but we do it for an eternal prize. So I run with purpose in every step. I am not just shadow-boxing. I discipline my body like an athlete, training it to do what it should.
> —1 Corinthians 9:25–27

At the end of his life Paul looked back on the race he had run. He had paid a high price for his loyalty to Jesus. In cities all across the Roman world he had been ridiculed, beaten, falsely accused, flogged, and impris-oned. Just before he died, he wrote Timothy, "I have fought the good fight, I have finished the race, and I have remained faithful" (2 Tim. 4:7). Jesus had told Paul he would suffer, and he did. Jesus told him he would stand before kings, and he did. Jesus promised to be with him through valleys of pain and on mountaintops of glory, and He was. Paul had been under no illusions. Following Jesus came at a steep cost of his reputation and his comforts, and he was willing to pay that price.

Christianity Lite overlooks clear—if uncomfortable—passages that tell us about the cost of genuine discipleship. When we follow Jesus, everything isn't always bright and sunny. We experience suffering, pain, and loss. Think about it. If God's design is to "[conform] us to the image of His Son" (Rom. 8:29, NKJV), we have to learn to give everything we have, just as Jesus did. Our suffering, though, is just a shadow of His. He suffered to pay for our sins and give us new life. We suffer so the pain can purify our hearts, deepen our dependence on God, and shine the light of His love and power to those around us. Jesus didn't preach a decaffeinated, low-cal, lite version of discipleship. He set the bar exceptionally high, and He never lowered it for those who want to follow Him.

DISTINGUISHING MARKS

The modern trend in American churches promises all the pleasures of the faith without any of the costs. We want every ounce of the benefits, but we don't want any hint of sacrifice. We pick and choose the passages that promise wonderful blessings, and we overlook or explain away those awkward statements such as the one about loving Jesus so passionately that every other relationship looks like hate in comparison. We want a wonderful marriage, but we don't want the burden of responsibility. We want a high-paying career without having to do too much work. We want kids who make us proud, but we don't want the risk that they might actually do things that would embarrass us.

It's not that hard to tell which tap we're drinking from. When we see clear directives in the Bible, do we obey or not? Do we tell the truth when honesty costs us something, or do we tell another lie? Do we reach out to help someone from another country, a single mom, or an elderly person—who can't

> We want every ounce of the benefits, but we don't want any hint of sacrifice.

give back anything in return—or do we ignore them and go on with our self-absorbed plans? Do we share some juicy gossip because it makes us look powerful and "in the know," or do we have the integrity to shut up? Do we use anger to intimidate someone weaker, or do we engage, ask questions, and listen? Do we read books and listen to preachers who tell us only what we enjoy, or do we have the guts to expose our hearts to the grown-up challenge of obeying God even when it hurts? The list of opportunities to display the life of the Spirit is almost endless, and it's not hard to spot the real thing.

The principles of cost and sacrifice aren't new to us. They exist in every sphere of life. If we want healthy bodies, we have to expend effort to exercise and eat healthy foods. That means we pick broiled chicken instead of deep fried, and we choose brussels sprouts instead of french fries. It doesn't take a genius to figure this out, but it certainly requires self-discipline if we're going to meet our goal. In the same way, there are truths in the Bible we may not like reading and hearing, but we must incorporate them if we're going to be spiritually healthy and effective children in God's kingdom.

We are masters at making excuses. It's comical to hear the creative reasons people are overweight. I know. I've been there. I don't like to do sit-ups. My flesh would far rather rock back in my recliner than do a bunch of sit-ups. One day when I was dreading this exercise, I started blaming God for putting my toes so low on my body. If they were higher, sit-ups would be a lot easier!

On the day Jesus told the crowd to count the cost, He realized they had completely misunderstood Him and His mission. They were following Him, that's true, but they were following for the wrong reasons. They wanted the blessings of Jesus more than Jesus Himself. They were mesmerized by His miracles. They enjoyed eating free lunches, watching healings, and hearing Him tell stories. But He wanted more from them than a warm body sitting on a hillside. Numbers didn't matter to Jesus. He gave them a gut check. He was more interested in pure and unfettered devotion...even if there were only a few who were willing to count the cost and love Him with all their hearts. It's the same today. His gracious invitation is for everybody, but only a few will take His hand.

When we write the definition of a disciple, we make it easy. We make the door really wide and the requirements simple. The concept, though, isn't ours to define. It's up to God to define the concept and establish the requirements. He has only one condition: We have to put Him above everything. No exceptions. Everything. If someone doesn't want to follow Him on His conditions, He doesn't glare at them in contempt and curse them. He's deeply saddened, and He watches as they walk away. But if we honestly count the cost and get on board, He's thrilled! He'll move heaven and earth to prepare us for the greatest adventure life can offer. Like all adventures, there will be danger, risk, and setbacks. But there will also be the wonder of seeing God work in and through us to change lives for eternity. The question for all of us is this: Is it worth the price?

Changed lives. That's what people are looking for. If our lives aren't transformed by the power of God, people have a right to wonder if we know Jesus at all. The distinguishing mark of a true disciple isn't perfection—that will be ours in the new heaven and new earth, but not now. The mark of a genuine follower of Jesus Christ is a changing heart, developing attitudes, and radically different behavior. When we are vitally connected to Jesus, He turns resentment into compassion, indifference into love, stinginess into generosity, worry into peace, hurriedness into patience, superiority into humility, and spinelessness into courage. It doesn't happen in an instant, but it happens...slowly and inevitably.

Or are we just about the show? Some of us would be happier if a bunch of angels appeared at church, over-whelmed people by their brilliance and beauty, and did miracles among us. What if that happened? Imagine those angels slaying hundreds in the Spirit, half the congregation speaking in tongues and the other half interpreting, people healed of diseases, and prophetic words being given to people in need. That would be fantastic, wouldn't it? If all that happened but people weren't any different in their homes, businesses, and schools the next day, it would all be a fantastic farce. People in our communities may be amazed by dramatic displays of God's power, but it won't make a dent if we haven't counted the cost, faced the test of character, and allowed God to change us from the inside out. If there's no change of our attitudes, language, integrity, and behavior, people have every right to wonder if our faith makes a difference at all.

> If our lives aren't transformed by the power of God, people have a right to wonder if we know Jesus at all.

FOUR COSTS

We can identify the cost of following Jesus in four broad categories: pride, comfort, habits, and reputation. Let's look at these.[1]

Following Jesus costs us our pride.

The Pharisees were absolutely convinced they were good enough to earn their way to heaven. They crossed every T and dotted every I to be sure they could stand before God and say, like the Pharisee in the Jesus's story, "I'm glad I'm not like those sinners. I tithe, fast, and do everything God wants me to do. I'm blameless!" The closer we get to the white-hot flame of Jesus's holiness and love, the more we see how far we fall short. A person who is perceptive and honest is more like the tax gatherer in the story who bows low, beats his breast in repentance, and says, "God, have mercy on me, a sinner!" (See Luke 18:9–14.)

Think of the disciples. They were with Jesus all day every day for more than three years, but when He needed them, they ran like little girls. When they took an honest assessment of their condition, they had to admit they had failed miserably—which made them perfect candidates to experience the magnificent grace of God.

Following Jesus costs us our comfort.

The metaphors used for true believers in the New Testament are important. We are called "servants," "athletes," "farmers," and "soldiers." In each of these roles people sacrifice comfort for a greater cause. They don't sacrifice because they're sadomasochists who enjoy pain. Not at all. Their eyes are fixed on something far higher, far nobler, and far more fulfilling than temporary pleasure.

In today's society we live in a cult of convenience.

Much of what we buy and many of the choices we make each day are designed to make our lives as comfortable as possible. There's nothing wrong with comfort...in its rightful place. But there's something terribly wrong about Christian servants, athletes, farmers, and soldiers choosing the couch over training and choosing entertainment over effectiveness in God's service.

Following Jesus costs some of our habits.

When we choose to live in the presence of God, the blazing light of His purity and love exposes habits we've considered normal for years. We realize all those times we've gossiped about people wasn't so amusing to God. It was sin. As we read God's Word with a heart to obey, we find passages about the tongue, sex, money, integrity, food, time, forgiveness and bitterness, and all kinds of other things. We realize we've excused destructive habits for decades. Now we make some new choices. We're determined to avoid dishonoring the One who gave Himself for us.

Following Jesus costs us our reputation.

When we are completely dedicated to Jesus Christ, He changes our hearts, our attitudes, and our choices. We become honest instead of shading the truth, we show kindness to people we previously overlooked, we're radically generous with our money and time, we forgive those who have hurt us, and we take the risk of being hurt again. When we choose to follow Christ and love Him with our heart, soul, mind, and body, some people around us will stand up and applaud, but some will laugh at us and ridicule us. They ask, "How can you be so stupid?" In fact, they may conclude that we've lost our minds.

People thought Jesus was crazy too. They looked at how He loved outcasts, and they concluded He was too soft. They saw how He stood up to the religious establishment, and they thought He was too harsh. He was so zealous for God's reputation that He stormed into the temple and overturned the tables of the greedy merchants who had no business setting up shop in God's house. Jesus wasn't what anyone expected Him to be, and it cost Him dearly. Before He was arrested, Jesus warned His men, "Do you remember what I told you? 'A slave is not greater than the master.' Since they persecuted me, naturally they will persecute you. And if they had listened to me, they would listen to you. They will do all this to you because of me, for they have rejected the one who sent me" (John 15:20–21).

Paul told the Galatians that there are no gray areas. We either live for the approval of people or the approval of God. Most people, including most who call them-selves Christians, are far more concerned with their reputation among their peers than God's evaluation of them. Paul drew a line in the sand: "Obviously, I'm not trying to win the approval of people, but of God. If pleasing people were my goal, I would not be Christ's servant" (Gal. 1:10).

In all four areas the cost is steep, and most people simply aren't willing to pay it. Jesus understood that fact. He didn't beg people to follow Him, and He didn't lower His standards so more would meet them. The standard was—and is—the willingness to die to our flesh so we can truly live.

MODERN EXAMPLES

I have the greatest respect for men and women in the military. The movie *Saving Private Ryan* is fiction, but the film's message of sacrifice is woven deeply into the fabric of every military life. Those in the military counted the cost of suffering and death before they signed up, and they put their lives on the line every day. Soldiers go through rigorous boot camp to prepare for combat. Fighter pilots train to avoid surface-to-air missiles and engage in dogfights with enemy aircraft. Sailors learn the fine craft of running enormous ships with phenomenal weapons so they'll be effective when they're called on. All these people live by a code far different from the self-focused way most people live: duty, honor, country. They give their hearts, their blood, and their lives for a cause and for their buddies. I'm not talking only about those who have won the Medal of Honor. I'm talking about those whose names you and I have never heard, the men and women who serve tirelessly and thanklessly because they're completely devoted to their mission. They are examples for all of us—especially for those who claim to follow a higher commander and a higher calling.

Not long ago I read a story about a pilot who was shot down in one of our wars in the Middle East. He was injured and immobile, and he was terrified of falling into the hands of enemy combatants, who would mercilessly torture him before cutting off his head. Special ops forces were sent to find and rescue him. They located his beacon, dropped in, and got him out before the enemy could target them. When he came home to recuperate, a reporter marveled at his courage. He responded, "I was only doing my duty. That's what I was trained to do. Nothing special." He didn't gripe about what happened to him. He didn't complain that it was unfair for the air force to send him into hostile territory. He knew that was what he had signed up to do. He didn't threaten to sue the government for his wounds, and he didn't insist on an increase in his salary to compensate for his trouble. If he had said any of this, his buddies would have gotten to him first and said, "What are you talking about? You signed up for combat duty. You knew it was possible to be shot down, wounded, captured, or killed. Don't criticize the air force, the soldiers who rescued you, or the doctors who put you back together. It was all part of the deal you signed."

No, the pilot would never have made those accusations or claims, so his buddies wouldn't have to correct him. Should we be any different? Is our calling to duty, honor, and God any different from the pilot's loyalty to his country? Christians today are soft. We complain at the slightest disappointment. We criticize God if we suffer any inconvenience. If we want to be real disciples of Jesus Christ, we need to take off our diapers, develop a backbone like a crowbar, and put on the full armor of God.

God wants to make us into soldiers. He has no plans to let us remain spiritual babies. Soldiers don't debate whether they are going to obey their commanding officer. They don't say, "Well, wait a minute. I'm not sure I want to do that after all. I'll let you know." No, all you hear from a soldier is, "Yes, sir." In boot camp one fact is drilled into the minds of the recruits: the military owns you. It's the same for us. Paul said, "You do not belong to yourself, for God bought you with a high price. So you must honor God with your body" (1 Cor. 6:19–20).

I love our republic. America is a fantastic country. But the primary allegiance of Christians isn't our republic—we live under the theocratic rule of Almighty God. Our King lives, He rules, and He expects to be obeyed. We have every right in our country to overturn laws and throw out leaders we don't like. With God it's different. We don't have the right to second-guess Him, obey only what we like, and disregard His rightful rule. We don't own ourselves; He owns us. We aren't the owners of our houses, cars, and kids; they're His. He is our King and our Commander in Chief, and we're His soldiers. When He gives a command, it doesn't matter what we think. We obey. We may ask how or when, but not if. If we've counted the cost, the question of if has already been answered.

In some churches and books remaining a spiritual infant is actually encouraged. Infantilizing the faith is a bad idea. Yes, Jesus said we are to have child-like faith—simple, pure, and joyful—but we aren't to remain childish. Paul instructed the Ephesians (and by extension, us) to grow up:

> Then we will no longer be immature like chil-dren. We won't be tossed and blown about by every wind of new teaching. We will not be influenced when people try to trick us with lies so clever they sound like the truth. Instead, we will speak the truth in love, growing in every way more and more like Christ, who is the head of his body, the church. He makes the whole body fit together perfectly. As each part does its own special work, it helps the other parts grow, so that the whole body is healthy and growing and full of love.
> —EPHESIANS 4:14–16

We are children of the King, but we are to grow up to be adult children who can handle responsibilities the King gives us. If we act like babies, He can't give us much. If we become mature, strong, growing men and women of faith, He'll consider us His valued part-ners. And someday we'll hear those magnificent words, "Well done, good and faithful servant. Enter into the joy of your Master!" I want to hear those words. How about you?

BREAKING THE YOKE

When the people of Israel were still wandering in the wilderness before they entered the Promised Land, God told them, "I am the LORD your God, who brought you out of the land of Egypt so you would no longer be their slaves. I broke the yoke of slavery from your neck so you can walk with your heads held high" (Lev. 26:13). Many people today are living under yokes of enslaving addictions, despair, bitterness, greed, lust, debt, and hopelessness. The weight of these things almost has a physical effect, causing them to bend over under the strain. God has broken the yoke of slavery to sin. We don't have to live under the oppression of sin, doubt, and worry any longer. The price has been paid.

Only the blood of the Savior can forgive sin. Paul wrote often and powerfully about crucifixion—Christ's and our identification with Him. Our salvation has, in one sense, already been completed, but in another way, making it real in our lives every day is an ongoing process. Crucifixion is essential in both. In Romans Paul talks about both past and present crucifixion. Let Paul explain. He wrote, "We know that our old sinful selves were crucified with Christ so that sin might lose its power in our lives. We are no longer slaves to sin. For when we died with Christ we were set free from the power of sin" (Rom. 6:6–7). That's past tense. Our sinful selves were crucified, dead, and buried with Christ. We're free! But any thinking, feeling, self-aware Christian knows that we haven't experienced complete freedom yet. Our old selves are still alive and kicking, so they need to be crucified every moment of every day. A couple of chapters later Paul explains that we "put to death the deeds of [our] sinful nature" every time it arises in our lives. (See Romans 8:12–14.) In my life the Holy Spirit whispers, "Glen, that attitude stinks," or "You're doing it again," or "That was so selfish." At that moment I choose between death and life. I choose a kind of death if I ignore the Spirit's prompting, blame someone else instead of taking responsibility, or convince myself it didn't matter. I choose life if I say, "Lord, You're right. That was sin. Thank You for forgiving me. I'm choosing to turn from that behavior. Help me, Lord."

If we want to be Jesus's disciples, we need to deny ourselves (which means to say no to our fleshly lusts and desires), take up our crosses, and die every day. That's exactly what Paul is describing in his letter to the Christians in Rome. Every time an impure, selfish, resentful thought comes out of our hearts, we grab it and kill it. How? By the power of the Spirit—living by His truth, His strength, and His grace. These choices don't happen once a week. They happen dozens of times every day (and some would say dozens of times every hour). As we soak our minds in the Word of God and let the Spirit of God work in us, these moments become clearer. We aren't surprised when God shows us our depravity and selfishness. We're still fallen people living in an evil world, but we have the Spirit of God living in us to give us the power to slay every sinful thought, attitude, and action as they surface.

The difficulty, of course, is that sin doesn't look evil and wrong—unless we see it in someone else. In our lives it appears to be benign, attractive, and even indispensable. How could we live without it? We're so familiar with our sins that they seem second nature. That's the problem! We need to be ruthless about every sin God shows us.

Are you eaten alive with envy because someone has something you think you deserve? Admit it, kill it, and replace it with God's peace and security. Are you haunted by daydreams of revenge because someone hurt you? Confess it, slay it, and let the forgiveness God has given you melt your heart so you actually love that person. Are your thoughts consumed with lust? Admit it, kill it, and let God fill the emptiness in your heart with the thrill of knowing and following Him.

Christianity Lite tells us we can make deals: "Just give up a little something—anything—to show you mean well." We turn off our computers so we don't look at porn, but we don't worry about the hatred that has been poisoning our hearts for years. We give some money to show that we're a good person, but we don't see any need to deal with our envy of people who have more than us. We'll go to church twice this month, but we don't have time to open our Bibles. We pick and choose which of God's directives we want to obey, and we make deals with God. We offer Him a few things, but we insist on holding on to others. We're sure that's enough to earn His blessings.

If we're serious about following Jesus, nothing is off limits. We hold nothing back. He doesn't want any of it unless we're willing to give Him everything we have:

the good, the bad, and the ugly. Many of us have a secret fantasy that we have a hard time letting go. We may be willing to let go of resentment, but not our right to be lazy. We may be willing to let go of laziness, but not the desire to pay somebody back for the hurt they've inflicted on us. We may be ready to do business with God about every area in our lives... but one. Jesus wants it all. How do we know what "it" is? It's the thing you're thinking of right now as you read these words. It's the secret you aren't willing to bring out into the light, the attitude that feels too good to give up, the habit that gives you power over others, the reputation that causes people to think you're something special.

Crucifixion is excruciating, but it's the only path to a resurrection.

Abraham had something he cherished more than God. It was his son Isaac. By the time the boy was twelve, he had taken God's place in the old man's heart. We don't know how many times God tried to reason with Abraham about this sin of idolatry. All we have is the account of God telling the old dad to take his son to a mountain and kill him. Kill him? The child of the promise? The one Abraham and Sarah had waited for so long? Yes, him. Kill him.

The old man took his son to the mountain, built an altar, tied his son on it, and raised his knife to kill him. At that moment God intervened and stopped him. Now God knew that Abraham's heart had been purified. It took drastic measures, but it worked. Abraham's heart was now completely God's.

What is the Isaac in your life? What do you cling to, protect from God's reach, and cherish more than anything in this world? Is it your kids, your spouse, your career, your hobby, your reputation, your freedom, your money, or something else? Whatever it is, let go of it right away, or God will ask you to take it to the mountain and kill it. This won't be a casual request. It's a holy command to get rid of anything that competes with God for top priority in your life.

That's what it means to count the cost.

That's what it means to crucify the flesh.

That's what it means to slay your idol.

That's what it means to kill your Isaac.

The decision to obey God is the commitment to align your life with God's decisions. We don't argue, we don't complain, and we don't try to make deals. We just say, "Yes, Sir."

Does the cost seem too high? Does following Jesus seem too demanding? If it doesn't, you don't understand what He requires. Following Him with your whole heart isn't hard; it's impossible! We can't do it by turning over a new leaf, trying harder, or gritting our teeth. To follow Jesus, we need a supernaturally transformed heart. We need the wonderful love, grace, and acceptance of God, and we need the power of the Holy Spirit to work in us and through us. Nothing else will do.

When we count the cost, we trust God to use us in others' lives. Lite Christians' hearts don't break when they see the needs of others. They aren't sources of light in the darkness around them, and they aren't salt to add flavor to every situation and relationship. They taste lukewarm to Jesus—which means they're running the hot faucet and the cold faucet at the same time. Jesus says turn one off, or He'll spit them out of his mouth.

God's invitation is warm and wide, but His demands are sharp and high. If we aren't willing to pay the price, we cannot be Jesus's disciples. If we're willing to take His hand, He promises to unleash in us the awesome power that created the universe and raised Jesus from the tomb. If we're cowards, we'll miss the adventure— the risks and the rewards. It's our call.

Worth It?

Instinctively we ask a simple but profound question when we face any transaction: Is it worth the price? People in business do a cost-benefit analysis to determine the validity of every deal. Soldiers fight to save the lives of their comrades and rid the world of evil men. Olympic athletes devote years of incredible discipline, sweat, and pain knowing that only a few of them will stand on the podium and hear their national anthem. Kids who play football—from Peewee Leagues to the NFL—spend countless hours working out, learning plays, and practicing so they can do their best. But only a few raise a trophy or wear a ring at the end of the season. People sometimes talk about the difference between luck and talent in sports, but great athletes know that they get a lot more "lucky breaks" if they practice harder. The reward for intense, single-minded dedication, however, isn't always tangible. It's the deep friendships formed in combat and competition, the deep satisfaction of knowing we've done our best even if we don't stand on the podium, and the affirmation of our commanders, teachers, and coaches. And God has promised to meet us at our point of suffering, heartache, and need. In fact, we can be thrilled in both blessing and suffering because both of them point us to Jesus.

Believers have a higher, better reward than servants, athletes, farmers, or soldiers. In the pivotal moment in *Saving Private Ryan*, Captain Miller tells the private, "Earn this." In our case Jesus doesn't tell us to earn anything. Our motivation isn't to earn His sacrifice but as a grateful response to it. We count the cost of discipleship, but only after we realize Jesus counted it first. We pay a price, but only because He paid it in full. We love because He first loved us.

Before the Incarnation Christ lived in fabulous riches and stupendous beauty in heaven. He stepped to earth not to be served but to serve. He was the King of glory, but He was ridiculed, tortured, mocked, and murdered. He became poor to make us spiritually rich.

We can never "earn this." The gift of grace is far beyond anything we can ever imagine, but we have eternity to think about it and let it sink into our hearts. "Before the Throne of God Above" is a beautiful song that was written over a century ago, but it recently surfaced again. It describes the sacrifice of Christ and our grateful response. Two of the stanzas say:

> Because the sinless Savior died
> My sinful soul is counted free.

For God the just is satisfied
To look on Him and pardon me.
Look on Him and pardon me.

One in Himself I cannot die.
My soul is purchased by His blood,
My life is hid with Christ on high,
With Christ my Savior and my God!
Christ my Savior and my God![2]

Does the incredible pardon of Jesus thrill you? If it does, the requirement to count the cost seems completely reasonable. If not, it sounds absurd. Paul summarized the rational response to Christ's sacrifice in his letter to the Corinthians: "Christ's love controls us. Since we believe that Christ died for all, we also believe that we have all died to our old life. He died for everyone so that those who receive his new life will no longer live for themselves. Instead, they will live for Christ, who died and was raised for them" (2 Cor. 5:14–15).

Look at Jesus, count the cost, and live for Him. It's the only decision that makes sense.

Years ago I made the choice to put Jesus first in my life. I've never doubted that decision for a single day. There have been plenty of times I've been confused, and there have been times when I didn't see how God was going to turn heartache or evil into good...but He did. I've never regretted my decision to count the cost and call Jesus my Master.

I'm confident He'll be a gracious and powerful Lord in your life too.

CONSIDER THIS...

1. What did Jesus mean when He said we can't be His disciples unless we "hate" everyone in our families, and even our own lives?

2. Do you agree or disagree that we're a nation of softies and quitters? Explain your answer.

3. How are soldiers and athletes good examples of people who count the cost? How would you describe their choices and motivation?

4. What are some specific ways following Jesus costs us our pride, our comfort, our habits, and our reputation?

5. Why do you think many Christians remain spiritual and emotional infants? What does it take to grow up and replace our diapers with the armor of God?

6. Why doesn't it work to make deals with God, giving up some bad habits but protecting our right to others? What does this perspective do to our relationship with God?

7. Why is it essential to remember that Jesus counted the cost and paid the price first?

8. What has God been saying to you as you read this chapter? What price do you need to pay? Are you willing to pay it? Why or why not?

five

SAVED WITHOUT OFFENSE

*Sometimes your medicine bottle has on it, "Shake
well before using." That is what God has to
do with some of His people. He has to shake
them well before they are ever usable.[1]*

—VANCE HAVNER

THE BIRTH OF a child—especially a first child—
is a glorious occasion. Everybody is excited to
bring the new baby home and then to church
for the first time. Mothers flock around the new mom
and talk about how beautiful the baby is (even when
there is considerable evidence to the contrary). Even
dads puff up their chests as they show off their new
son or daughter. It was no different in the first century.
When Joseph and Mary brought the infant Jesus to the
temple, they offered the only sacrifice they could afford:
a pair of pigeons. They were thrilled to have their new
son in the worship service! But in every part of Jesus's

life light was mixed with darkness, and joy was tainted by sorrow.

From God's point of view Jerusalem was the most spiritual city on the planet, and the temple was the holiest place anywhere. That's where heaven and earth met. On that day Joseph and Mary brought Jesus to dedicate Him to God, but only two elderly people recognized Him as the promised Messiah, the Savior of the world. They were Simeon and Anna. Why weren't there a parade and refreshments? Why weren't there banners and balloons? Because the Son of God didn't come in the way people expected. It wasn't a grand, lavish show. He came with humility and grace.

Simeon was an old man who faithfully came to the temple every day. The Holy Spirit had promised that someday he would see the Messiah. He didn't want to miss that! Finally it happened. He saw the young couple and their baby, and the Lord told him, "He's the one!"

The old man took the baby in his arms and thanked God that the Light of the world had finally come. He understood the Messiah's expansive role. He prayed, "I have seen your salvation, which you have prepared for all people. He is a light to reveal God to the nations, and he is the glory of your people Israel!" (Luke 2:30–32).

Joseph and Mary were amazed. Someone else knew about their Son! Now, wouldn't you think it would have dawned on them that their child was special? After all, an angel had appeared to Mary, she was a virgin when she conceived, and all the prophesies in the Bible pointed to this child being the long-awaited Messiah! Still they were amazed that this old man recognized Him.

Simeon then turned to Mary and spoke words that must have chilled her heart: "This child is destined to cause many in Israel to fall, but he will be a joy to many others. He has been sent as a sign from God, but many will oppose him. As a result, the deepest thoughts of many hearts will be revealed. And a sword will pierce your very soul" (vv. 34–35).

Wherever Jesus went—from the time He was an infant until He rose from the hill back into heaven— He was a fork in the road: some people loved Him, but many were offended by Him. His message was unmistakable. Imagine what Mary must have been thinking at that moment. Simeon was saying that this dear little baby, the promised Messiah of God, was going to offend people, irritate them, and confuse them. Who wants to be corrected? Jesus's life and message never left people the same. He graciously welcomed all who came to Him, but He never left them in their previous condition. His arms were open wide, but He demanded complete loyalty and obedience. He spoke glowingly of God's love, but He made sure people understood the cost of obeying Him. He often confused those who followed Him, and He infuriated those who opposed Him. At one point (in John 6) the only ones who chose to remain with Jesus were the twelve disciples. The rest became angry and walked away.

If we don't feel offended by God from time to time, it's not the real God we're following. If we don't feel confused by Him, we don't realize that His infinite wisdom is far beyond human comprehension. If we don't have spiritual anxiety at the demands of discipleship, we haven't really heard His clear command to follow Him into sacrifice and suffering. Jesus gave all, and He demands all. That's a chilling prospect, even for the bravest among us.

We get offended because God doesn't do what we think He should do. Many of us signed up with Jesus for an easy life and lots of blessings. Suffering? Not on our list. Sacrifice? Maybe for somebody else. Waiting on answers? We want our blessings now! Anything less than a life of perfect peace, wonderful blessings, and abundant prosperity hacks us off. After all, we deserve it, don't we?

DUMBING JESUS DOWN

In his book *Finding God* author and Christian psychologist Larry Crabb observed, "We have become committed to relieving the pain behind our problems rather than using our pain to wrestle more passionately with the character and purposes of God. *Feeling better has become more important than finding God.* And worse, we assume that people who find God always feel better." The result is that we treat God like "a specially attentive waiter." When He gives us good service, we give Him a tip of praise. When He doesn't immediately meet our every need, we complain.[2]

With piercing insight into our culture, Notre Dame sociologist Christian Smith observes that people today have a view of God that can be characterized by "Moralistic Therapeutic Deism." In other words, following rules is important because it guarantees that God will make us feel better, but actually it's an arm's-length relationship with a God who is "out there somewhere." Smith's study focused on adolescents but extends to the wider culture of our society. He notes:

> We get offended because God doesn't do what we think He should do.

> Moralistic Therapeutic Deism is...about providing therapeutic benefits to its adherents. This is not a religion of repentance from sin, of keeping the Sabbath, of living as a servant of a sovereign divine, of steadfastly saying one's prayers...of building character through suffering, of basking in God's love and grace, of spending oneself in gratitude and love for the cause of social justice, etc. Rather, what appears to be the actual dominant religion...is centrally about feeling good, happy, secure, at peace. It is about attaining subjective well-being, being able to resolve problems, and getting along amiably with other people.[3]

This is Christianity Lite in a nutshell. It focuses on the friendly, pleasant, fun, accepting, and exciting aspects of Jesus's life and message, but it ignores the parts that make us feel uncomfortable. In today's "seeker-friendly" churches and books only half the gospel is taught—because people want to hear only the pleasant part of Jesus's message. These pastors and authors use the Bible, they encourage people to pray, and they tell great stories of God's blessings, but they downplay Jesus's demands. God, we're convinced, is just like us. As the philosopher Voltaire once noted, "If God created us in his own image, we have more than reciprocated."[4]

I'm not suggesting that we need to lay grace aside and impose oppressive rules on anyone. That's not the gospel, either! We need a full-orbed gospel message—the one Jesus taught, modeled, and imparted to His disciples. Anything else leaves us with a saccharin-sweet taste in our mouths but feeling empty. A lite version of the gospel simply can't satisfy the deepest needs and longings of the human heart. We can't be truly saved by a "Lite Savior." We need the Lamb of God to die for us, but He's also the Lion of Judah who demands everything we have as we follow Him.

Real faith in Christ is infused with the Holy Spirit's power, not just self-effort. It requires concerted prayer because that's how we connect with God's heart, power, and purposes. It comes at great cost because it asks us to crucify our flesh so we can experience the life of Jesus in us. And it means we are often pushed and corrected because we're deeply flawed. The gospel of Jesus offends us...deeply...and often.

Sooner or later Jesus gets under our skin. No matter

who we are, what titles we hold, and how long we've gone to church, the demands of discipleship become too much to bear. John the Baptist had dunked Jesus in the Jordan and watched as the Holy Spirit descended on Him like a dove. When John was facing death, he sent his followers to ask Jesus if He was really the Messiah. Jesus sent word back, "Yes, My miracles testify about who I am. You can count on it." Then Jesus told John's men, "And blessed is he who is not offended because of Me" (Matt. 11:6, NKJV). Even John was on the verge of being offended by Jesus's claims. He needed to be reassured so he could face death with confidence.

We like the glowing promises, but we feel deeply offended by Jesus's demands. Deny ourselves? No, we'd rather indulge ourselves. Pick up our cross? We prefer to buy the newest gadgets, kick back and watch television, and go on nice vacations. Die daily? That can't be in the Bible, can it?

> A lite version of the gospel simply can't satisfy the deepest needs and longings of the human heart.

Hebrews 11 is the "Hall of Faith." It recounts all the times when God came through to rescue people from persecution, pain, and death. We read about Abraham, Joseph, Moses, Rahab, and the prophets. The stories build to a crescendo of God's blessings: shutting the mouths of lions, escaping fire and sword, and even raising people from the dead! But the accounts don't end there. It goes on to say:

But others were tortured, refusing to turn from God in order to be set free. They placed their hope in a better life after the resurrection. Some were jeered at, and their backs were cut open with whips. Others were chained in prisons. Some died by stoning, some were sawed in half, and others were killed with the sword. Some went about wearing skins of sheep and goats, destitute and oppressed and mistreated. They were too good for this world, wandering over deserts and mountains, hiding in caves and holes in the ground.

—HEBREWS 11:35–38

Many people read this passage and shake their heads. "Surely," they wonder, "something is wrong with the people described in this passage. Did they forget to claim God's promises? Did they harbor secret sins? Was God asleep when those people suffered so cruelly? Did He abandon them?" No, they suffered because they fully trusted God. He was there working out His divine, mysterious purposes, just as He's in the middle of our lives when things don't go the way we hoped. God promises to meet our needs, not satisfy our wants. He often rescues us through the storm, not out of it. We can get offended and angry when He doesn't give us the blessings and rescue we expect. When we feel offended and disappointed, we need to look deeper into the character of God.

When we suffer, we look around at others who seem to have an easy life, and we feel cheated. Comparison kills. It poisons our minds and hearts because it makes us feel superior (when God supernaturally rescues us) or inferior (when He rescues someone else but not us).

Most of us have a very low threshold of pain. The modern, lite version of Christianity completely erodes our tolerance to suffering of any kind. In prolonged periods of history the church endured severe persecution, and in fact, believers in certain nations of the world today experience fierce persecution. Would we stand strong for Jesus if we really suffered as Christians? Would we speak out boldly for Christ if we faced expulsion from our communities? How many people would show up at prayer meetings if we faced jail for praying? Do we have the love and courage to keep talking about Jesus if the authorities or our neighbors threatened to kill us? Would we even keep giving to the church if the government changed the tax laws and charitable donations were no longer deductible?

Are we willing to suffer—at all—for our faith? Many of us aren't strong. We're easily offended when we feel "pressured" to step out of our comfort zones in any way. Our view of the Christian faith is that it's supposed to make us feel good. If it demands anything significant and requires sacrifice, we're outta there!

THE TRAP

In "seeker-friendly" churches people are convinced of God's promises, but they don't recognize the call to be loyal no matter what the cost. They read about God being Jehovah Jireh, and they're offended if God doesn't provide for every need immediately. They find a passage describing God as Jehovah Shalom, but they're offended because they're in the middle of life's problems instead of enjoying perfect peace. They see He's Jehovah Rapha, and they complain about being sick. They find Scriptures about God as Jehovah Rohi, but they don't see His protection in their lives. When God doesn't come through as they expected, they get offended, and then they either shake their fist at Him in anger or walk away in despair.

Are we any different?

Paul told the Corinthian church that the gospel of Jesus was offensive to the Jews and foolishness to the Gentiles (1 Cor. 1:23). The Greek word for "offense" is *scandalon*, which is the part of an animal trap that gets tripped so the trap springs and captures its prey. Any time we grab an offense, our false expectation traps us. The faulty promise of perfect peace and plenty drew us into the trap, and our demand for a cost-free life springs the steel jaws. How do we act when we're trapped? The same way an animal responds when it's captured. We fight back, we wrestle, and we try to get out. Some animals have been known to chew their leg off to get free from a snare. I've seen people who blamed everybody in the world, including God, for their problems instead of learning the lessons God wanted to teach them through suffering. They were deeply offended that God didn't do what they expected Him to do.

We feel offended by big things and little things. When people genuinely hurt us and betray us, we want revenge. Have you noticed how many movies and television programs are based on the demand for payback? Those shows reflect the hearts of the audience: "If you hurt me, I'm going to hurt you." "You stole from me, so I'm going to make you pay." "If you lie about me, I'm going to spread all kinds of slanderous gossip about you." That's the way of the world, but it's not the way of Jesus. He said to love people, even our enemies…to forgive and seek reconciliation…to put bitterness away from us and pursue peace in our relationships.

But it's not just the big things that raise the hair on our necks. When we feel pervasively offended, we get upset about the smallest things. I've watched people in the express checkout line at the grocery store. Some people count the items in the person's basket in front of them. If the sign says "Limit: 10 Items" but that lady has twelve, it's Armageddon right there in the grocery store! "Technical foul! This woman has too many things in her basket. I'm outraged! Get the manager over here right now. Where's the rope for the lynching?"

When we're easily upset about things going wrong in our lives, the cycle is self-feeding: We become even more self-absorbed and self-righteous. We play the role of victims, and we demand that everybody on the planet jump to make us happy—which, of course, doesn't work out very well, which causes the cycle of demands and despair to continue.

JESUS OFFENDS OUR PRIDE

We have an idea of what God should do for us, but we also have a definite picture of how God's messengers should look and act. I face this every weekend. People used to dress up to come to church, but not as much anymore. My children have questioned my Sunday attire. They want me to be more casual, more approachable in my choice of clothes when I preach. I sometimes wear jeans and a nice shirt, but most of the time I still wear a jacket. My kids think I'm way out of style, but sometimes an older person will corral me and whisper, "Pastor, where's your tie? You should be wearing a tie, you know." I can't win.

After Jesus sent word back to John the Baptist that His miracles were proof that He was the promised Messiah, He turned to talk to the crowd. John had his expectations of the Christ, and the crowd had expectations of their spiritual leaders. John didn't fit their image at all. Jesus asked them, "What kind of man did you go into the wilderness to see? Was he a weak reed, swayed by every breath of wind? Or were you expecting to see a man dressed in expensive clothes? No, people with expensive clothes live in palaces. Were you looking for a prophet? Yes, and he is more than a prophet" (Matt. 11:7–9).

The people were used to seeing the nicely dressed Pharisees and the elegantly robed Sadducees around town. These religious leaders always looked sharp. Their robes were fresh from the dry cleaners, and every fold was neatly ironed. John looked a little different.

He looked like Chuck Norris at the end of one of his movies after he'd been in twenty fights. John's robe wasn't dry-cleaned. It wasn't even dry. It had honey and locust stains. His hair hadn't been washed since the last time he was in the Jordon baptizing somebody. He looked bad, and he smelled worse. How could God use a man who looked like this?

Jesus continued to correct their misperceptions. He told them, "John is the man to whom the Scriptures refer when they say, 'Look, I am sending my messenger ahead of you, and he will prepare your way before you.' I tell you the truth, of all who have ever lived, none is greater than John the Baptist. Yet even the least person in the Kingdom of Heaven is greater than he is!" (vv. 10–11).

Jesus blew their perceptions out of the water. He said, "John is God's man. He may offend your pride. You think you deserve somebody more elegant, but you don't. You laugh at John, but he's the greatest man who ever lived. Can you handle that?"

What do you criticize? What do you gossip about? What makes you feel superior to "those people"? In church we complain about the preacher's appearance, the stories he tells, his wife's clothes, the songs, the worship leader being too demonstrative or not passionate enough, the length of the service, parking, and everything else imaginable. When many of us read the Bible, we don't pay attention when we find God's requirements and demands. We only pay attention when it says things that benefit us and promise to make our lives easier and more fun.

In His defense of John the Baptist, Jesus wasn't quite through. He told them, "And from the time John the Baptist began preaching until now, the Kingdom of Heaven has been forcefully advancing, and violent people are attacking it" (v. 12). We're in a war, and in combat, people get dirty and wounded, and sometimes they die.

The kingdom of God is not made up of thumb-sucking, immature, diaper-wearing snowflakes that disappear when the going gets hot.

We're soft. We get our feelings hurt so easily. When John was in prison, he was offended that he was in jail but Jesus was outside preaching the gospel. Jesus was his cousin, but He didn't even come to see him in prison. John was hurt, and he was angry. His wounded feelings caused him to doubt Jesus. That's when he sent his disciples to ask if He was really the Messiah. Jesus used John's doubts as a mirror to reflect the fact that John offended the crowd. It appears that everybody was offended! That's the point. Offenses are windows into our hearts. Disappointments can reveal our deepest desires and expectations. If our hopes line up with God's values and purposes, we'll handle suffering with calm assurance that God will work everything out for good according to His eternal purposes. If our hearts don't line up with God's, we'll complain, gripe, lash out, and run away. And we'll keep looking for somebody to tell us what we want to hear.

IT ONLY TAKES ONE

In many cases people can be faithful friends, spouses, children, or church leaders for years, but if they don't meet our expectations—just once—they fall from our good graces. They may have been there for us hundreds of times, but one perceived failure is all it takes to change our minds. That happened to Jesus in some of His closest relationships on earth. Jesus had three friends who lived in the little town of Bethany outside Jerusalem: Lazarus and his sisters, Mary and Martha. Jesus enjoyed going to their home, where He could relax. One day the sisters sent word that Lazarus was very sick. They knew He could heal their brother, so they asked Him to come. Jesus didn't go. He waited two more days, and then He led His men to Bethany.

When they approached the town, Lazarus had been dead and in a tomb for four days. A crowd of mourners was at the sisters' house. When they got word that Jesus was coming, Martha went out to see Him, but Mary stayed in the house. Mary was deeply offended that Jesus hadn't come earlier—and it cost the life of her brother. Can you imagine what was going on in her mind? She was probably thinking, "We've done so much for Jesus, but when we needed Him, He didn't even come. He could have healed Lazarus, but now he's dead. Martha can go out to see Him if she wants to, but not me! I don't care about all those miracles He did for other people. He didn't come through for us when we needed Him!"

Mary didn't come out to meet Jesus until Martha

talked with Him and sent word that Jesus asked to see her. She may have been hurt and angry, but she went to talk to Him. That's an important point about being offended by Jesus: we can't do much to change our feelings, but we can obey in spite of them. Mary had a choice: she could have continued to sulk in her home, or she could respond to Jesus's invitation to meet with her. She went out, talked to Jesus, and witnessed the miracle of Lazarus being raised from death to life.

We won't see miracles if we stay trapped in our offended feelings. We have to get up, move toward Jesus, and trust Him no matter what happens. Quite often the real miracle occurs in our hearts, turning sour to sweet, doubt to faith, and complaints to gratitude.

FINDING HOPE IN OFFENSIVE LANGUAGE

At one point Jesus wanted to take His men away from Palestine, so they traveled north to the Phoenician coast. News about Him had spread even there. A Gentile woman had a daughter who was cruelly possessed by a demon. She found Jesus and begged Him to cast the demon out of her child.

Uncharacteristically, Jesus didn't even reply. The disciples were annoyed by her neediness. They told Jesus, "Tell her to go away. She is bothering us with all her begging."

Jesus finally spoke to the woman: "I was sent only to help God's lost sheep—the people of Israel." When she wouldn't stop asking for His help, He told her, "It isn't right to take food from the children and throw it to the dogs."

This seems like the most callous language...coming from Jesus Himself! Jewish people of that day often insulted Gentiles by calling them "dogs." This term refers to wild, mongrel scavengers, not beloved pets. Jesus used a different word that means "little dogs," but He still called the woman and her daughter dogs! He was testing her to see if she'd still trust Him.

The woman responded, "That's true, Lord, but even dogs are allowed to eat the scraps that fall beneath their masters' table." She passed the test.

We can almost hear Jesus laugh when He replied, "Dear woman, your faith is great. Your request is granted." And her daughter was instantly healed. (See Matthew 15:21–28.)

How many of us would have stormed out the door when Jesus compared us to dogs? We have thin skins, so we take offense at almost anything.

The woman who came to Jesus had plenty of reasons to be offended: She was a Gentile and a woman, Jesus and his men were on vacation and didn't want to be bothered, and she could have been branded a "bad mother" because her daughter was infested with a demon. All she needed, though, was a glimmer of hope. Jesus had tested her, and she believed. He rewarded her faith and tenacity by casting the demon out of her daughter.

Jesus's answer implied, "Thank you for not being offended. Thank you for looking past My words and into My heart. You handled criticism better than anyone I've ever seen. In fact, I would like to teach Dr. Know-it-all and Sister Wonderful about responding in faith instead of feeling offended so easily."

Today we multiply potential offenses. We get upset about race, denominations, language, politics, where people live, how they talk, their kids, their lifestyle, their nation of origin, what they wear, how they eat, and all kinds of other habits. God doesn't prefer a certain color of skin or people who support a particular policy or candidate. He looks into our hearts, and He offends us to expose what's really there. If we're too easily offended—a condition revealed by griping and feelings of superiority or inferiority—we need a refresher course on the grace of God. We're hopelessly lost sinners who are only saved by the blood of the righteous Son of God. Our race or nationality doesn't matter. We all came out of the same sewer of human depravity. One of us isn't more special than another. We're all equally in desperate need of the grace of God, and we're all equally loved, forgiven, and accepted by Christ. Grace triumphs over petty offenses.

FAMILY OFFENSES

Some of the most painful wounds inflicted on us come from those closest to us—our family members. The Gospels record an event that must have hurt Jesus deeply. He had been healing people and teaching the crowds. His popularity was soaring...but not with those who should have known Him best. Mark tell us:

> One time Jesus entered a house, and the crowds began to gather again. Soon he and his disciples couldn't even find time to eat. When his family heard what was happening, they tried to take him away. "He's out of his mind," they said.
>
> —MARK 3:20–21

His own family thought He was insane! But this evaluation didn't stop Jesus. He kept right on teaching, healing, and casting out demons. Soon His family came to see Him again. They stood outside a packed house. They sent word for Him to stop what He was doing and come out to see them. When He got the message, He rhetorically asked the messenger, "Who is my mother? Who are my brothers?" Then He looked at those around Him and said, "Look, these are my mother and brothers. Anyone who does God's will is my brother and sister and mother" (Mark 3:33–35).

Many people start off strong in their commitment to Jesus, but family disapproval derails them. They don't have the strength to stand up to opposition, or even hard questions, and they feel deeply offended when their parents, spouse, or kids don't applaud their faith in Jesus.

Christ's message offended His family—and, it appears, even His mother, Mary. But He didn't let their negative reaction distract Him. Instead He valued the faithful men and women who were signing up for His sacrifice, His mission, and His message. They became His new family.

When the prophet Samuel went to Jesse's house to anoint the new king of Israel, Jesse paraded all of his sons in front of him—all but one: David. Jesse didn't even consider his youngest son part of the family. Later, when David became king and wrote many of the psalms, he reflected, "Even if my father and mother abandon me, the LORD will hold me close" (Ps. 27:10).

It hurts when our families offend us, but we can be confident that Jesus is proud of us. In Him we have unconditional acceptance, complete security, and a much bigger family with far more brothers and sisters.

OFFENDED BY GRACE

We claim to be people of grace, but are we? The Pharisees believed they were the protectors of God's name, God's cause, and God's law, but they didn't understand Jesus at all. They were deeply offended by almost everything Jesus said or did. He healed a man with a crippled hand on the Sabbath, and they went Old Testament on Him! He stood up for a woman caught in adultery—not her sin, but her dignity as a person. He went out of His way to meet with a Samaritan woman who was drawing water from a well. But she was no ordinary outcast. She had been married five times and was living with the sixth man. Most people considered her worthless, but Jesus considered

her a treasure. When Jesus was at a Pharisee's house
for dinner, a prostitute who had been saved came in
uninvited to express her love by pouring perfume on
His feet and wiping them with her hair. The Pharisee
was horrified that Jesus let a woman like that touch
Him! Over and over again the religious leaders were
outraged because Jesus warmly welcomed prostitutes,
tax collectors (who were considered traitors because
they collected money from other Jews for the Roman
government), women, children, foreigners, and every
other kind of outcast. He even touched stinking lepers
to communicate His healing love!

The religious elite had the Bible, they followed the
traditions, and they met at the temple every time the
doors were open. Zeal wasn't their problem, but they
didn't understand the concept of grace. They measured
spirituality by how well people kept rules; Jesus measured it by mercy, justice, and gratitude.

They weren't just annoyed by Jesus. They hated Him.
Grace threatened them, and in the end, they plotted
to kill Him. Offended by grace? Yes, in the worst way.

Are we any different? How do we react when a
person unlike us responds to the grace of God? Are
we thrilled, or do we find fault in them? Do we cel-
ebrate like crazy, or do we keep them at arm's length?
Do we have a checklist to determine if they're acceptable? Do we focus on the things we don't like about
their skin color, the way they talk, their income level,
or their part of town? Or do we realize Jesus has
broken down the dividing wall that separates us from

one another. We're all part of God's family...whether we like it or not.

FOLLOWING AT A DISTANCE

How can you tell if Jesus has offended you? There may be dozens of signs, but I think one is the most common. On the night Jesus was arrested, everything went south for the disciples. Only a few hours earlier they had been arguing about who would be the greatest in Jesus's cabinet when He inaugurated His kingdom—and they expected it to happen the next day! When He was arrested, they were confused and frightened. All their hopes were blown to pieces. Their dreams exploded.

One of them—Peter—had promised he would remain faithful even if all the rest ran away. Matthew tells us:

> Then the people who had arrested Jesus led him to the home of Caiaphas, the high priest, where the teachers of religious law and the elders had gathered. Meanwhile, Peter followed him at a distance and came to the high priest's courtyard. He went in and sat with the guards and waited to see how it would all end.
> —MATTHEW 26:57–58

Distance. It can happen in every kind of relationship: marriage, parenting, friendships, business, clubs, sports teams, and neighborhoods. When people feel offended, they back away from the one who hurt them.

They may create this space because they're so mad they don't want to interact, or they may be protecting themselves from being hurt again.

We go to great (and sometimes amusing) lengths to avoid any contact with the person who hurt us. In our homes we avoid eye contact; we talk to everybody else—including the dog—before we'll talk to that person. We orchestrate our every movement all day to stay out of sight. When we sit down to dinner, not a word passes between us. Even if the salt is right in front of the one who hurt us, we ask a child on the other side of the table, "Johnny, would you please pass me the salt?" You could cut the tension with a dull knife, but nobody has the guts to say, "Hey, what's going on here?"

Whenever we feel offended, we put distance between us and the one who hurt us. It's human nature, but it's lethal if we don't address it.

It happens all the time in spiritual life. Disciples who are offended may keep following, but they put some distance between themselves and Jesus.

There are millions of people in churches today who were offended in the past and backed away from Christ. They felt close to Him, but He failed to live up to their expectations at some point, and they separated their hearts from Him. They still go to church, tithe, and serve in all kinds of ways, but their hearts aren't fully His any longer. And, of course, many offended believers find churches where no one asks too much of them. No demands, no call to obedience, no sacrifice. Christianity Lite seldom offends.

If we're serious about being Jesus's disciples, offenses are inevitable. We get offended when we realize God demands that we die daily to our selfish desires and live fully for His honor. We're offended by plenty of people at work, in our neighborhoods, and even under our roofs who think we've lost our minds because we love Jesus more than pleasure, comfort, power, possessions, and reputation. Our devotion to Christ seems so weird to them, and they delight to tell us we're nut cases. But that's not all. Plenty of people in churches are offended by our passionate, unrestrained commitment to Christ. Maybe they feel guilty, or maybe they feel jealous. Whatever the reason, they delight in tearing us down so they can feel superior to us.

BEYOND OFFENSES

We don't expect our casual friends, the coffee club, and golf buddies to offend us. We hang out together because they make us feel good. If something happens and things get tense, we move on and find other friends. After all, our friends have no right to offend us.

Too often we have the same perspective of Jesus. If we call Him our friend, we don't think He has any right to offend us. Yes, He's a friend, but not like any other friend we've ever known. He is the Lamb and the Lion, the Alpha and the Omega, the Creator and sustainer of life, the great I Am who existed before time began. He is the potter; we are the clay. We don't come to Him on equal terms. He owes us nothing. Jesus Christ loves us so much He stepped out of heaven to suffer injustice and cruelty so He could pay the price we could never pay for our sins, and He welcomes us as His own.

He wasn't just offended when He came to earth; He was crushed. He didn't just have His feelings hurt; He was murdered.

We've been bought with a steep price. He has every right of ownership. We are no longer our own; we belong fully to Him—body, soul, mind, skills, gifts, time, relationships, and possessions.

Whenever we feel offended by Jesus, we're forgetting this fundamental fact. When we remember Jesus's sacrifice, *we welcome His correction* because we know He needs to refine us so He can use us for His higher purposes—much higher than our personal peace and prosperity. *We welcome suffering* because we realize it's the classroom where we get in touch with God's heart and learn the most important lessons in life. *We welcome seasons of waiting* because we're sure God is never in a hurry to accomplish His divine will in us and through us.

Without an understanding of the cost of discipleship, people are offended by all of these difficulties because pain and waiting don't fit into their carefully constructed set of expectations about a life of blessings. We need to ask some hard questions: Is the pupil greater than his teacher? Should we expect an easier life than the One who died and rose for us?

When our selfishness and pride offended Jesus, He forgave us. When people offend us, we need to draw from the deep well of God's forgiveness so we can extend forgiveness to them. When we realize we've offended Jesus yet again, we confess our sin, thank Him for His boundless grace, and put Him back in the center of our hearts. Discipleship begins by accepting God's gift of forgiveness, but it doesn't end there. For the rest of our lives the grace we've experienced deepens and matures so that we have the power to forgive those who hurt us, and we realize—again and again—that the sacrifice of Christ has ransomed us from hell and given us a reason to live. Nursing offenses is one of the enemy's traps that keep us in bondage to old hurts. Forgiveness releases us from the trap. We don't wait until the person asks for forgiveness or promises to never hurt us again. We forgive the way Jesus forgave us. Author and pastor Lewis Smedes commented, "To forgive is to set a prisoner free and discover that the prisoner was you."[5]

A heart full of grace and gratitude is seldom offended by the demands of the gospel. To a true disciple, those demands make perfect sense. We obey not to earn brownie points or impress the people who are watching us, but because we want to honor the one who paid the ultimate price to rescue us from hell, adopt us into His family, and make us partners in bringing God's kingdom to earth.

Does Jesus offend you? Or are you so thrilled with His love, forgiveness, and power that you're willing to charge into the depths of hell to please Him? It's the only reasonable response to His great grace.

CONSIDER THIS...

1. Do you agree or disagree with Larry Crabb's observation that for many in the church, "feeling better has become more important than finding God"? Explain your answer.

2. How would you define and describe "Moralistic Therapeutic Deism"? What is the impact of this perspective on a vibrant life of faith?

3. Who were the people who felt offended by Jesus? How did they respond to Him?

4. In what ways are offenses "traps"? How do they keep people locked into negative perspectives and habits?

5. How was John the Baptist offensive to the people around him? How did he feel offended by Jesus? How did Jesus reassure him?

6. What about Jesus is (or has been) most offensive to you? How did you respond to the perceived offense?

7. How does going deep into the grace of God give us a different perception of offenses?

8. Does Jesus have the right to demand love and loyalty from us? Why or why not?

six

SAVED WITHOUT SERVICE

Life's most persistent and urgent ques-
tion is, "What are you doing for others?"[1]
—MARTIN LUTHER KING JR.

"I'M TOO BUSY."

"Not now. Maybe some other time."

"No, I'm not interested."

"Surely you can find somebody more qualified."

"I'm already doing too much."

"I've got an appointment to have my nails done. Sorry."

"I'd love to, but I don't have time."

"What's in it for me?"

When people need us to step up and help, we're masters at finding excuses. Our default mode is "Life is all about me," and helping others doesn't fit into our priorities. So thanks, but we'll pass this time.

There was a time in the church when helping people

wasn't just a nice thing to do—it was a matter of life and death. Historians tell us that two plagues ravaged the Roman world in the second and third centuries. Each time between a quarter and a third of the entire population perished. The first began in AD 165 when Marcus Aurelius was the Roman emperor. It may have been the world's first smallpox epidemic. In fact, the emperor was one of the plague's victims. The second devastated the empire beginning in 251. This time it may have been measles.

In each of these devastating plagues the pagans prayed to their gods, but people kept dying. They looked to their doctors for help, but the doctors left town to save their own skins. Family members ran for their lives and left infected brothers, sisters, parents, and children to die alone. Without the most basic nursing care, most of those who contracted the diseases died horrible deaths.

The Christians, though, didn't run out on their families. They stayed and cared for them. And they went to the houses of the pagans to care for them too. A church leader, Dionysius, explained their motivation:

> Most of our brother Christians showed unbounded love and loyalty, never sparing themselves and thinking only of one another. Heedless of danger, they took charge of the sick, attending to their every need and ministering to them in Christ, and with them departed this life serenely happy; for they were infected by others with the disease, drawing on themselves

the sickness of their neighbors and cheerfully accepting their pains. Many, in nursing and curing others, transferred their death to themselves and died in their stead.... The best of our brothers lost their lives in this manner.[2]

These humble, caring Christians loved their sick neighbors as themselves. They reached out to help "the least of these," and God used them to save the lives of millions of people—often at the cost of their own lives. In *The Rise of Christianity* Rodney Stark concluded that the loving service of the Christians during these two plagues caused the number of believers to explode in the Roman Empire. How did it happen? Christians cared for their own family members instead of leaving them to die, so their mortality rate was much lower. And the pagans, whose lives were saved by the gentle, loving care of Christian neighbors, suddenly became very receptive to the message of the gospel. They had seen Christ's love in action! Within two centuries the number of people who claimed to be Christians grew from less than 1 percent to more than 25 percent. Because Christians risked death (and often suffered death) to serve people in their communities, Christianity became the dominant faith of the Roman Empire.

The spread of Christianity, according to Stark, wouldn't have happened if the believers hadn't risked their lives to serve sick people around them.[3]

EMPTY WORDS

In Christianity Lite people talk often about the love of God. All the pious words and platitudes taste great, but they're less filling—they don't call people to a full-hearted devotion to Christ and His cause. Most believers are familiar with James's statement in his letter: "So you see, faith by itself isn't enough. Unless it produces good deeds, it is dead and useless" (James 2:17). Many people read this and think, "Cool. I'm good. I put five dollars in the offering plate last month. That's a good deed. And I didn't shout driving tips to that woman who cut me off in traffic. Man, that's a really good deed. OK, I'm good to go."

What was James really talking about? What kind of deeds demonstrate authentic faith? The context of the passage gives us the answer. He had just said that when we see someone without clothes and food, it's not enough to walk by and wish them well. We stop and meet those needs—no matter how inconvenient it may be and how much it costs. Real faith is always demonstrated in acts of sacrificial service. But we need to be careful. We don't serve to be noticed and patted on the back. We serve quietly, with no fanfare, anonymously if possible, expecting nothing in return. We serve this way because that's the model of Jesus Christ.

THE SERVANT

In his letter to the Philippians Paul told them, "Don't be selfish; don't try to impress others. Be humble, thinking of others as better than yourselves. Don't look out only for your own interests, but take an interest in others, too. You must have the same attitude that Christ Jesus had" (Phil. 2:3–5). Is that even possible? It's our nature, our basic instinct, the default setting of the human heart to look out for ourselves at all times and in all ways. Paul instructs us to live in a way that is diametrically different. For us to give instead of taking, love instead of demanding, and serve instead of insisting on being served, our hearts have to overflow with the love and power of Jesus.

> Real faith is always demonstrated in acts of sacrificial service.

Paul didn't say it would be *nice* to have the attitude of Christ. He said we *must* have this mind-set. If we're going to become fully devoted disciples, there's no other option. We have to be internally transformed—in our thinking, our values, and our motives—so we become servants like Jesus was.

How far did Jesus stoop to serve? Paul paints the picture for us:

> Though he was God,
>> he did not think of equality with God
>> as something to cling to.
> Instead, he gave up his divine privileges;
>> he took the humble position of a slave
>> and was born as a human being.
> When he appeared in human form,
>> he humbled himself in obedience to God
>> and died a criminal's death on a cross.
>> —PHILIPPIANS 2:6–8

Jesus didn't show up and demand attention. He was born in a stable, and His first crib was a feeding trough. As an adult He went from town to town caring for people, healing the sick, and teaching about the kingdom of God. When He became popular, He told people He healed not to tell anybody! He was worthy of angelic praise and adoration, but He felt completely comfortable sitting around a campfire each night with a bunch of guys who couldn't figure out who He really was. When He was arrested, He said He could have called ten thousand angels to wipe out the human race and stop His suffering, but He chose to humble Himself to the greatest extent: love propelled Him to suffer a criminal's death of shame on a Roman cross.

I've known plenty of people who were glad to serve...as long as they got plenty of recognition. They claimed to be great singers and even told me God wanted them to sing at our church. I told them God hadn't shared that information with me. Some have informed me they have the gift of healing and wanted to perform miracles in our church. I told them to care for people in the hospital and the street. If people are humble enough to serve without recognition, God will give them a platform.

We have to be very careful about our motives for serving. If we do it for fame, to earn points, to gain power, or even to be noticed, we've missed Jesus's attitude. Author Os Guinness asks penetrating questions about our motivations. We may be working very hard, but for selfish reasons. "Do we enjoy our work, love our work, virtually worship our work so that our devotion to Jesus is off-center? Do we put our emphasis on service, or usefulness, or being productive in working for God—at his expense? Do we strive to prove our own significance? To make a difference in the world? To carve our names in marble on the monuments of time?"[4]

We may want acclaim for our acts of service, but we need to leave the recognition in God's hands. Our task is to serve gladly in obscurity and let God handle the honors. While Jesus was on earth, a few people recognized Him and loved Him. Most were confused or offended by His selfless sacrifice. But the Father noticed. Paul explains God's response to Jesus's sacrifice:

> Therefore, God elevated him to the place of
> highest honor
>   and gave him the name above all other
>   names,
> that at the name of Jesus every knee should
> bow,
>   in heaven and on earth and under the earth,
> and every tongue confess that Jesus Christ is
> Lord,
>   to the glory of God the Father.
>   —PHILIPPIANS 2:9–11

A sacrifice that costs nothing is worth nothing. A sacrifice performed to win applause vanishes into dust. But a sacrifice given for Christ's sake—and only for

His sake—wins the applause of heaven. People who drink Christianity Lite either don't want to be bothered with serving, give a little and expect a lot, or serve purely to be noticed by people.

There's another way. Again, Jesus points us in the right direction.

SEVEN PRINCIPLES OF SERVING

What would you do if your execution was scheduled for tomorrow? Would you party like crazy one last time, drift off into depressed oblivion, call a friend, or find a good book to help you pass the time? We know exactly what Jesus did on the night before He was crucified. He showed His disciples what it means to serve. John puts us at the scene:

> A sacrifice that costs nothing is worth nothing.

Before the Passover celebration, Jesus knew that his hour had come to leave this world and return to his Father. He had loved his disciples during his ministry on earth, and now he loved them to the very end. It was time for supper, and the devil had already prompted Judas, son of Simon Iscariot, to betray Jesus. Jesus knew that the Father had given him authority over everything and that he had come from God and would return to God. So he got up from the table, took off his robe, wrapped a towel around his waist, and poured water into a

basin. Then he began to wash the disciples' feet,
drying them with the towel he had around him.

—JOHN 13:1–5

From Jesus's example we find seven important
principles.

1. The hour had come.

Whenever Jesus talked about His "hour," He was
referring to the time of His death. After all the miracles and teaching, the time had come for Him to go to
the cross to die for the sins of the world. It was why He
came to earth in the first place.

In the same way the hour for our death has come
too. We won't die a literal death on the cross, but if
we want to be Jesus's disciples, we choose to die every
day to our sinful passions and fleshly desires. As we've
explained before, Jesus didn't come to hurt us; He
came to kill us. When we die to our selfishness, we can
really live. Jesus couldn't be raised from the dead until
He died. In the same way we can't experience the full-
ness of spiritual life unless we crucify the flesh. How
does this happen? Paul wrote to the Galatians, "Those
who belong to Christ Jesus have nailed the passions
and desires of their sinful nature to his cross and crucified them there. Since we are living by the Spirit, let
us follow the Spirit's leading in every part of our lives"
(Gal. 5:24–25).

When we crucify our natural desires for glory, power,
control, and pleasure, we replace those things in our
hearts with God's pardon, peace, and purpose. It's a

pretty good swap! So the first principle of becoming the servant God wants us to be—becoming a little more like Jesus—is to recognize that death leads to life, and crucifixion leads to resurrection. This is the hour for us to die. Actually, it's *always* the hour for us to die.

2. Love has no end.

Has there ever been a more faithful, loyal friend than Jesus? The men who were with Him at this last dinner were incredibly disconnected—just like you and me. They argued about who was the greatest, and they jockeyed for position—just like us. Their hearts were clouded by selfishness, and they looked down on people who weren't like them—just like you and me. Still, Jesus never gave up on them. He didn't throw up His hands and walk away. He was fiercely loyal to them even after this night when one betrayed Him, another denied Him, and the rest (except John) ran for their lives.

As His disciples, with the Spirit of God living in us, we follow His example: We don't give up on people who are slow, stubborn, and selfish. We speak the truth to them, we correct them, and we affirm them passionately—but we never give up on them.

Many of us give up on people if they hurt us. If that's the case, we won't have any meaningful relationships because sooner or later every human being will let us down. We need to forgive as Jesus forgave, love as Jesus loved, and accept as Jesus accepted people—with a boatload of grace, kindness, and patience. There's no Plan B. We don't bail out when someone is unkind to us. We're in a covenant relationship with God and with His people. These are our brothers and sisters, and we'll be with them for all eternity. (That fact may not be comforting for some of us.) We need to overlook annoyances and forgive genuine offenses...and have the wisdom to know the difference. We can hold people accountable—not to punish them, but out of love, because it's best for them to be honest about their flaws. Love people until the end. That's how Jesus loves you and me.

Isn't that the kind of friend you want? Isn't that the kind of friend you need to help you through the rough spots in life? Isn't that the kind of friend people need you to be for them?

3. We will be shocked by betrayal.

If we protect ourselves from getting too close, we'll limit our vulnerability, but we'll forfeit depth and intimacy in our relationships. Being vulnerable is essential, but it comes at a cost. Sooner or later we'll suffer the sting of betrayal. Someone we trusted will turn his back on us, gossip about us, or try to ruin our reputation. It happened to Jesus, and it will happen to us.

There are no guarantees. We can't orchestrate our lives so that we'll never be hurt again. If we live in this world, we'll get hurt from time to time. If we don't expect it, we'll be devastated. If we're wise and strong, we'll certainly be hurt, but it won't destroy us. This is real life, not some kind of fairy tale. Betrayals happen.

When you make a decision to love people, you empower them to hurt you. Love necessarily makes us

155

vulnerable, and the closer the relationship, the more vulnerable we are. The person who has the most power to hurt me is my wife. I've let her in as close as I possibly can. She has enormous power in my life to build up or tear down. And I have power in her life because we're close. It's like we each have knives in our hands. We can use those knives to carve something beautiful, or we can use them to stab, gouge, and destroy. That's how vulnerable we are.

When I talk about the necessity of being vulnerable, many people shake their heads. They tell me, "Pastor, I've been vulnerable before, and it didn't work out. I can tell you this: I'm never going to let anybody hurt me again!"

Well, that's their decision, but it's one that puts severe restrictions on their ability to give and receive love for the rest of their lives. Self-protection has some value, but it comes at a very high price. It limits love and makes them utterly miserable.

God has made us relational beings. We were meant for love. Sure, it's a risk, but refusing to take a risk— with God and with people—eliminates the greatest source of joy and meaning in our lives. When we're betrayed, we have a reason to get even. Everything in us cries out for revenge! But Jesus chose to forgive instead of blasting us into an alternate universe. When people hurt us, we need to look deep into the well of our experience of God's amazing grace so we can extend grace to those who inflicted us with pain. Paul wrote, "Get rid of all bitterness, rage, anger, harsh words, and slander, as well as all types of evil behavior. Instead, be kind to each other, tenderhearted, forgiving one another, just as God through Christ has forgiven you" (Eph. 4:31–32). That's how to handle betrayal.

The devil loves divisions in the family of God. When we nurse hurts and refuse to forgive, Satan laughs and applauds. He's won the battle! We need to realize that the devil and his dark angels are the source of bitterness, resentment, and betrayal in God's family. He reminds us of all the times that person has let us down, and we question every word the person ever spoke to us. Before long we live in a poisonous cloud of resentment, doubt, and plots of revenge. But we go to church with a smile on our faces. That's the level of duplicity in our hearts.

For Jesus, the devil had already put it in the heart of Judas to betray the Lord of glory for a few silver coins. Notice where Judas was. Jesus hadn't kicked him out. Judas was sitting at the table having dinner with the one he was going to betray. Jesus knew what was coming, but He continued to extend His hand of grace.

4. Know who you are.

When He faced betrayal, darkness, and death, Jesus still knew exactly who He was. He never doubted He had come from God and was going back to God. If Jesus Christ needed to remember His identity, we need this assurance far more. We are sinners saved by grace. We were lost but have been found. We didn't do anything to twist God's arm or impress Him with our brilliance. We came to Him with empty hearts and open arms, and He filled them both by His great grace. Now we have the ultimate purpose any person can ever receive: we have the unspeakable privilege of representing the King of kings to the people of the earth! That's our high calling and responsibility. He could have given that privilege to angels, but He gave it to you and me. Amazing.

If we don't know our identity in Christ, we'll be constantly insecure and full of self-doubt. In our desperate need to be accepted we work compulsively to *prove* we're worthy of praise, we *please* people to earn their approval, or we *hide* to keep them from knowing how flawed we really are. We buy the right clothes, drive the right car, get the right position at work, and live in the right neighborhoods so people will think we're cool. In church we want to serve where we'll be noticed. We wear masks to pretend we have it all together, but we're dying inside. We're terrified somebody will know we're phonies.

The devil loves to whisper in our ears, "You're not getting enough recognition." "Those people don't appreciate all you do for them." "You can do a lot better than that person. You should be promoted." Comparison is a delicious but deadly dessert. When our identity is based on positions, possessions, and approval, we listen to the devil's whispers and get upset by them. But if our identity is rooted and grounded in the unconditional acceptance of God, we won't pay attention to these lies. We don't need to try to *be* somebody in the eyes of people because we already *are* somebody in God's sight.

More money doesn't make us wiser or better people. If we're dumb with ten dollars, we're still dumb with a thousand. And winning the lottery doesn't change our spiritual IQ. People measure each other by their bank accounts, but God looks at our hearts. That's a more accurate indication of our character.

A genuine experience of the grace of God transforms our sense of identity. Grace makes us humble and confident. If we live in shame, we're humble but not confident. If we're proud, we're confident but not humble. Only the grace of God radically transforms our hearts because we realize we're so wicked it took the death of God's Son to pay for our sins, but He loves us so much He was glad to do it. God's grace is the source of true humility and real confidence.

You don't need to wear a particular brand of clothes, drive a fancy car, have a title, build a big bank account, or go on lavish vacations to impress anybody. The only one worthy of being impressed is God, and He's not interested in all those external things. All He cares about is your heart. If you want to impress Him, love Him with all your heart and serve Him gladly.

5. Be willing to be inconvenienced.

When I was young, mealtimes were almost sacred. When we sat down for dinner, the world could be coming to an end, but no one got up to check on it. I have a feeling that meals were just as important in Palestine in the first century. At the last dinner with His disciples Jesus broke tradition by getting up to serve the men at the table. He was willing to endure a hassle because love was more important to Him than convenience.

The essence of the Christian life is to be inconvenienced to help others—no matter what the cost.

What does it take for us to cross the threshold of inconvenience so we take action to help someone in need? I'm not talking about monumental needs, just normal ones. Your spouse calls to you from another room, "Hey, honey, would you help me with this?"

And you yell back, "Uh, not right now. There's fifteen minutes left until the game is over. Maybe Jimmy can help you."

We carve out our time, our space, our comfort, and we protect it as the Secret Service protects the president. "No one," we think (but we'd never say), "has the right to infringe on my sacred area. Not now, not ever. They can find somebody else to help them."

Here's a news flash: A true servant serves. He doesn't carve out areas that are off limits, and he doesn't jealously guard his "rights." When he becomes aware of a need, he jumps in to meet it...not with a grumble but with a smile. A servant doesn't have a checklist of criteria to see if the job fits perfectly. The task may not match the schedule, his gifts, or his resources. The one quality that characterizes a true servant is the willingness to help. If he has limits or deficiencies, he'll look for other resources to meet the need.

6. Wear the clothes of a servant.

When Jesus got up from the table, He didn't grab a microphone and deliver a monologue, and He didn't receive any awards. He took off His outer robe, wrapped a towel around His waist, poured water in a bowl, and began washing the disciples' feet.

We can be certain of one thing: the disciples were astonished. In that day a person's clothing indicated his status in society. Only the lowest servant wore a towel around his waist. The most humble slave or servant was assigned the task of washing the dusty feet of guests who came for dinner. Jesus was assuming that role in the lives of men who had walked with Him for more than three years, and He was humbly serving them on the night before He was going to pay the ultimate price. He was the Lord of glory, the subject of the angels' songs, but He was willing to become the lowest servant.

Most of us act in the opposite way. We put on clothes to look more important than we really are. We look for positions of status, rank, and acclaim. Our goal, our passion is to impress people so they'll think well of us. It would be one thing for this prideful positioning to happen in the world of business, entertainment, and sports, but too often it happens in church.

> The essence of the Christian life is to be inconvenienced to help others—no matter what the cost.

Because we are completely secure in our high position in Christ—we are chosen, adopted, blood-bought children of the King...what could give us more honor than that?—we should never consider ourselves better than anyone. If Jesus was humble enough to serve as the lowest servant, we can be willing to humbly and gladly serve anybody and everybody God brings into our lives. No one is off limits. Not black people or white people, Hispanics or Asians, liberal Democrats or Tea Party Republicans, those who smell pretty and those whose stink makes us gag, people who live under bridges and those who own mansions, people whose faith is just like ours and those who believe things that are very different, kids with tattoos and old people who shouldn't be driving anymore—God has given all of them to us. They are tests of the sincerity of our faith in Jesus. They are human beings who are treasures in God's sight.

I'm not above picking up trash at our church, and I'm not above helping around the house. No one has proclaimed me "king of the world." Jesus has called me His friend and His partner, so I want to follow His example of serving the way He served. I have a long way to go, but at least I'm on the road. The Lord of all was the servant of all. If I want to be His disciple, I need to follow in His footsteps. Can I borrow a towel?

7. Doing is louder than speaking.

In sports, teams often talk big and put other teams down. When I was younger, we didn't invent trash talk, but we perfected it. There came a point, though, that it was time to get on the field. Then talk didn't mean anything. It was "put up or shut up."

The same is true in our Christian lives. We can talk a good game about loving God, serving people, giving to the poor, and reaching the lost, but if we don't take bold action, it's all just empty words. I appreciate people who do more than they say. As a pastor my job is to talk, but I know that talking has its limits. The world won't be reached and God's kingdom won't come "to earth as it is in heaven" if all we do is talk it to death. We have to "put up or shut up."

In the first century the servant who washed guests' feet didn't tell jokes or share stories about his day. The people whose feet were being cleaned probably didn't even see his face. He just did his job quietly, anonymously, and effectively.

As you've read these pages about serving, what has God put on your heart? Have you thought of things you should have done but didn't? Did the Spirit give you a vision for helping someone? God's promptings are important. Don't ignore them. It may be as simple (and challenging) as walking into the kitchen to wash the dishes tonight—without being asked. Or it may be far more extensive, such as creating a ministry to care for widows, single mothers, sex slaves, or other members of the fraternity of "the least of these."

Don't talk it to death. Make your plans and pull the trigger. Take action to serve.

RESISTANCE, EMBRACE, AND DRIFT

As Jesus went from man to man washing the disciples' feet, He came to Peter. The fisherman instinctively understood that this wasn't the right role for the

Messiah. He asked, "Lord, are you going to wash my feet?" He implied, "No way I'm letting you do this!"

Jesus told him, "You don't understand now what I am doing, but someday you will."

Peter continued to protest, "No...you will never ever wash my feet!"

I can imagine Jesus smiled at His friend as He explained, "Unless I wash you, you won't belong to me."

That did it. Peter wanted to be all-in. He almost yelled, "Then wash my hands and my head as well, Lord, not just my feet!"

Jesus probably laughed and shook His head as He told him, "A person who has bathed all over does not need to wash, except for the feet, to be entirely clean" (John 13:6–10).

Now it was time for the object lesson. John tells the story,

> After washing their feet, he put on his robe again and sat down and asked, "Do you understand what I was doing? You call me 'Teacher' and 'Lord,' and you are right, because that's what I am. And since I, your Lord and Teacher, have washed your feet, you ought to wash each other's feet. I have given you an example to follow. Do as I have done to you. I tell you the truth, slaves are not greater than their master. Nor is the messenger more important than the one who sends the message. Now that

you know these things, God will bless you for doing them."

—John 13:12–17

Why do we serve? What is our motivation to give, care, pray, fast, and pour ourselves out for others? The point Jesus was trying to make was that we love because He loved us first, we forgive those who hurt us because He first forgave our sins, and we serve because He first served us. If our Christian activities are designed to impress people or earn points with God, they're worthless. But if they are the spillover of a heart filled with the love, power, and grace of Christ, they bring a smile to God's face. Jesus doesn't ask us to do anything He hasn't already done to the ultimate degree. He asks us to die to our sinful desires; He died for all mankind. He invites us to pray boldly; He and the Spirit pray for us all the time. He tells us to serve gladly and sacrificially, expecting nothing in return. That's how He lived, served, and gave Himself for us.

But I've always wondered...Jesus healed lepers, restored sight to the blind, gave sack lunches to tens of thousands, raised people from the dead, stopped hemorrhaging, and performed countless other miracles. In fact, John says his Gospel would fill every corner of the world if all the miracles were included in its pages! When Jesus hung on the cross, where were all these people? The only ones there were a few women and John. Where was Bartimaeus? Where was Lazarus? Where were the lepers who had been cleansed?

It's easy to stand up for Jesus when everything is

going well. Opposition, heartache, and suffering sift our hearts. Many who stand and sing praises in the good times vanish when trouble comes—especially when their reputations are threatened. It's a lot easier to give in to peer pressure and walk away from Christ than to cling to Him in love and loyalty.

Jesus loved people to the end, but most of them bailed out on Him. Still, a few weeks later, 120 people were together when the Holy Spirit fell from heaven like fire. It only takes a few to be the sparks to light a forest fire of grace, love, and power—but it takes a few.

Much of the time serving is fun. Sometimes it's grueling, thankless, and challenging. Jesus gave us an example of humility and tenacity. Will we follow Him? Will we be His disciples?

The apostle Paul learned to serve in good times and bad. Everywhere he went, some believed, some doubted and walked away, and some tried to kill him. As he approached Jerusalem after his third journey to take the gospel to the Roman Empire, his friends warned him not to go. He replied with clarity and courage:

> And now I am bound by the Spirit to go to Jerusalem. I don't know what awaits me, except that the Holy Spirit tells me in city after city that jail and suffering lie ahead. But my life is worth nothing to me unless I use it for finishing the work assigned me by the Lord Jesus—the work of telling others the Good News about the wonderful grace of God.
>
> —ACTS 20:22–24

In Christianity Lite comfort and reputation mean everything. If God will make us richer and happier, we're glad to follow Him. But Jesus and Paul had a very different agenda. They valued a treasure far more valuable than possessions, positions, and popularity—the applause of God. Nothing else came close.

Would you have been one of the people who was brave enough to show up at the cross that horrible day? Would you have been one of the 120 a few weeks later when the Holy Spirit fell with fire among them? Would you have stood with Paul and suffered beatings and stoning for your faith? What does it take for you to quit?

None of us, though, are expected to stand alone. Someone once said, "The spaces between your fingers were created so that others could fill them in." Do you have people who stand with you in times of suffering? Those people are treasures too.

People are watching. In the second and third centuries Christians served tirelessly, courageously, and gladly in times of plague. Many gave their lives for their neighbors. Did the pagans notice the love poured out for them by their Christian neighbors? You bet they did! And millions were drawn to Jesus. There's something about dying for others that gets people's attention.

Have the same attitude that Jesus Christ had. Love and serve to the end.

CONSIDER THIS...

1. What are some common excuses people (maybe even you) have used to get out of serving others?

2. What makes us think that convenience is a sacred right? What are some sources of this message?

3. What do you think prompted the believers in the second and third centuries to care for victims of plague, even at the cost of their own lives? Would Christians today be willing to make this kind of sacrifice? Why or why not?

4. The passage in Philippians 2 tells us about Christ's humility, sacrifice, and exaltation. How is this a model for us as we "have the same attitude"?

5. Which of the seven principles of serving (modeled by Jesus when He washed the disciples' feet) inspire you? Which ones challenge you? Explain your answer.

6. Why is the applause of God a strong, pure motivation to serve selflessly? How can we overcome our fleshly desires to value comfort, acclaim, and control above everything else?

7. Why is it essential to realize Jesus first served us before He asked us to serve Him and others?

seven

SAVED WITHOUT SHARING

*God uses people. God uses people to perform His
work. He does not send angels. Angels weep
over it, but God does not use angels to accomplish His purposes. He uses burdened, bro-
kenhearted, weeping men and women.[1]*

—DAVID WILKERSON

AT ONE POINT in His ministry Jesus spoke to two
very different audiences at the same time. Luke
tells us that outcasts—including prostitutes and
tax collectors—loved hanging out with Jesus. Outside
the circle of Jesus and the outcasts stood a bunch of
Pharisees. They despised the outcasts, and they couldn't
stand the fact that Jesus loved people they despised.
They were two groups as different as they could be. I
can imagine the sinners enjoying Jesus's company as the
Pharisees watched, snarled, and sneered. At the scene
you could cut the tension with a knife. Jesus used this
occasion to tell three stories about finding something

that had been lost: a sheep, a coin, and a son. In all three, when the lost thing was finally found, a party erupted!

THE LOST COIN

In the second story a woman lost one of her ten silver coins. Each coin represented a day's wage, so the one she lost was valuable. Jesus asks the obvious question, "Won't she light a lamp and sweep the entire house and search carefully until she finds it?" (Luke 15:8)

People hate losing things. I've seen people go to pieces when they lose their car keys, wallet, or purse. They search frantically, and the look in their eyes tells everyone, "Hey, you better find it for me or get out of my way!" When they find it, they can't wait to tell people. They were going to be late for an appointment, but now they can go. They were going to have to call the bank to replace their credit cards, but now they don't have to bother. They were going to lose pictures of the kids and grandkids (or the dog), but they have those treasures again. They're so excited they can't stand it!

That's the picture Jesus was painting about something that's lost and found. He explained what happened to the woman and her coin: "And when she finds it, she will call in her friends and neighbors and say, 'Rejoice with me because I have found my lost coin.' In the same way, there is joy in the presence of God's angels when even one sinner repents" (vv. 9–10).

Do you understand what Jesus is saying? When a

lost person is found, the angels in heaven don't shrug their shoulders and say, "Well, there's another one. Big deal." No, they break out the banners, cake, ice cream, and noisemakers. They throw a blowout party! That's the value of a single soul in the eyes of God.

The underlying message in Jesus's three stories was that the sheep, the coin, and the younger son represented the sinners sitting near Him. All of these outcasts were lost and needed to be found. Whose job was it to look for them? It was the responsibility of the religious leaders to "sweep the house" to search for them, but instead they stood back with their arms crossed, despising the lost people and the One who loved them enough to find them. Both groups understood the deeper message of the stories—one group loved it; the other grew red with rage. Before long the Pharisees plotted to kill Jesus.

THE LESSON OF THE WALLET

I got an idea of what Jesus meant in the parable of the lost coin when Debbie and I flew to Dallas to join my friend in dedicating his new church. After the celebration we stayed a couple of days to see the city. On Wednesday morning we got up early to pack and drive to the airport for our noon flight. Debbie and I folded clothes, put some stuff in bags, and slid shoes into our suitcases. I picked up the car keys, but I couldn't find my wallet. No problem. I was sure it was in the room somewhere. I checked my dirty jeans. Not there. Then I looked under the bed, in the bathroom, and on the desk. There are only so many places in a hotel room where things can hide, and I looked at all of them. No wallet. Now I kicked into panic mode! I told Debbie, "I've never lost my wallet! Never! Where could it be?"

I was concerned about the cash and credit cards, but even more, I realized my driver's license was in my wallet. If I couldn't find it, I couldn't get on the plane to go home. I'd be stuck in Dallas until the trumpet sounded and Jesus appeared in the clouds...or almost that long.

Debbie looked in the same places I'd already looked. (What do you do in a situation like that? Do you hope she finds it and makes you look dumb, or do you hope she doesn't find it...which makes you look dumber?) Debbie didn't find it. Suddenly she had an idea. She asked, "Do you remember that shop at the outlet mall?" I nodded. She was excited. She was sure she had figured it out. "Wasn't that the last time you had your wallet out?"

"Yeah!" I almost yelled. I looked at my watch. "We'd better get over there quick!"

We grabbed our bags, jumped in the rental car, and raced across town to the store. It hadn't opened yet, but I could see people stocking shelves in the back. I knocked on the door, but they were either deaf or were ignoring me. I knocked harder. Still no response. I felt like I was in *The Twilight Zone*. I started using the flat part of my hand on the glass so my ring made as much noise as possible. I banged so hard I thought the glass might break! Finally a lady walked to the door and opened it. Before she could tell me to come back later, I blurted out, "I think I left my wallet here when we bought something yesterday. There, I see the person who waited on us. Can I talk to her?"

I slid inside the door without being invited. With Debbie in tow I quickly walked over to the other clerk and said, "Do you remember us? We were here yesterday, and you waited on us. I think I left my wallet when I paid the bill. Have you seen it?"

She looked under the counter and shook her head. "No, it's not here."

I was desperate. "Is there a bin someone might have put it in?"

She looked at me and shook her head again, "No, you didn't leave it here."

I turned to Debbie and said dejectedly, "Let's go back to the hotel. Maybe it's there after all."

Our flight time was rapidly approaching, so I sped back to the hotel. We had already checked out, so we had to get hotel security to let us back into the room. We were frantic now. I looked everywhere in the room again, and we went through our luggage for the tenth time. I was hoping an angel had miraculously put my wallet in my dirty jeans. No, nothing there. Debbie was on the phone trying to get some kind of ID for me so we could fly home, and she called the banks to see if anyone was using our credit cards.

I was frustrated and demoralized. I picked up my briefcase to go through it one more time. I never put my wallet in my briefcase. As I opened it, I noticed a bulge in a side pocket. I unzipped it. To my shock angels began singing and clouds rolled back as my wallet appeared!

This event showed me the point of Jesus's stories about things that are lost and found: when I'm around lost people, I need to have the same urgency, passion, and dedication people saw in me when I lost my wallet.

Are people worth less than car keys, a wallet, a purse, a tool, or a golf ball? Do they deserve less attention and determination when they're lost? On another occasion Jesus asked, "And what do you benefit if you gain the whole world but lose your own soul? Is anything worth more than your soul?" (Mark 8:36–37). This means that the value of a single soul is far more valuable than all the accumulated wealth people pursue. In other words, if you had a balance, the "weight" of the most obscure, forgettable person on the planet is far "heavier" than all the gold, oil, real estate, diamonds, stocks, bonds, and other riches put together. Every person is supremely valuable to God, but every person is hopelessly lost apart from Jesus.

Are we anxious about people being lost? Do we lie awake at night wondering how to reach them? Do we agonize until they're found and saved? Are we even looking for them at all?

What do we value above all else? In the lite version of Christianity people see Jesus as their consultant but not their King. They see Him as their butler, maid, or cook—running around wearing a chef's hat and apron and waiting for their next command. When we only value Jesus for what He can do to make us happy and successful, we live to advance our careers and our reputations. We don't care much about the eternal destiny of others. But that's not real Christianity. When our hearts are filled with the grace and power of Jesus Christ, nothing matters but His honor—nothing. What breaks His heart breaks ours. The passions that drove Jesus drive us. When Jesus explained the value of a human soul, He concluded, "If anyone is ashamed of me and my message in these adulterous and sinful days, the Son of Man will be ashamed of that person when he returns in the glory of his Father with the holy angels" (Mark 8:38).

If we love Jesus more than anything, we'll never be ashamed of Him.

READING A LIFE

Jesus didn't come to earth to perform a one-man show. He came to rescue people from hell and begin a revolution. After the resurrection and before His ascension He told His disciples, "Go into all the world and preach the Good News to everyone" (Mark 16:15). One part of that equation isn't too hard. We're already "in the world." We rub shoulders with people at school, at work, in our neighborhoods, playing or watching sports, at the mall, on airplanes, and everywhere else. We're an incredibly mobile society, and we brush by people wherever we go.

Some Christians, though, avoid any contact with sinners. They find Christian plumbers, Christian hairdressers, Christian mechanics, and Christians in every other aspect of life. There's nothing wrong with using believers to provide quality services with integrity, but we need to be careful that we don't create a "holy huddle" and miss opportunities to be light in a dark world. Jesus told His disciples, "As the Father has sent me, so I am sending you" (John 20:21)—into the darkness to be light... onto the banquet table to be salt.

The second part of Jesus's final instructions to the disciples, though, is more of a challenge for those who drink Christianity Lite: they don't want to "preach." I'm not talking about standing in a pulpit and delivering a sermon—they have no intention of speaking up about Jesus in normal conversations.

> If we love Jesus more than anything, we'll never be ashamed of Him.

Why? Maybe they aren't convinced the gospel is really "good news." To them, maybe Christianity is just a long list of dos and don'ts, a strict moral code no one can meet. Or maybe a watered-down gospel seems irrelevant to their hopes, fears, and relationships.

If that's what we're to proclaim from the housetops, no wonder we're quiet! But that's not the real gospel. We have the life-changing, life-saving message of grace—nothing weak, nothing superficial, nothing phony. People aren't temporarily misplaced without Christ. They're hopelessly lost! They aren't good people who need a little help from God. They're hell-bound sinners who have no capacity to impress God on their own! We have no hope apart from the saving grace of Jesus.

Mark concludes his Gospel: "When the Lord Jesus had finished talking with them, he was taken up into heaven and sat down in the place of honor at God's right hand. And the disciples went everywhere and preached, and the Lord worked through them, confirming what they said by many miraculous signs" (Mark 16:19–20).

When did the Lord work through them? Only when they went out and told people about Jesus. When did they see many miraculous signs? Only after they got up and spoke out. They didn't sit around and say, "Well, if God wants to use me, I'm willing. I'll wait until He moves me. But if He doesn't move me, I guess it's a sign He doesn't want to use me."

Christians who don't go out of their way to seek the lost are anemic and self-absorbed—and maybe still lost themselves.

What do people see when they spend time with us? We may be turned off because "those people" curse, tell dirty jokes, or laugh at sin. Do they see us turn up our noses at them and condemn them? That's how the Pharisees treated the prostitutes and tax collectors. Or do they see us loving them with a powerful blend of grace and truth?

The people we walk past each day probably aren't reading the Bible, but they're reading our lives. We are "living epistles." What's the message we're communicating? To the people around us, we are their Scriptures. We display the character, love, and strength of Jesus. The question is: How accurately do our attitudes, reactions, and intentional choices represent the King of kings? Can people see even a little of Him in us?

TWO WEAPONS

John, the author of Revelation, was given a sneak peak into eternity. When the curtain was drawn back, he saw a war between God's angels and the demonic forces. Satan is called "the accuser." He stands before God as the district attorney listing every item on the indictment against every person on earth. We all stand accused of doing wrong, talking wrong, and being wrong—and the accusations are true. We're guilty.

But we aren't alone. We have an advocate in the courtroom. Jesus pleads our case—He doesn't claim that we're innocent, but He assures the righteous Judge that He has paid the price for us. John wrote:

> It has come at last—
>   salvation and power
> and the Kingdom of our God,
>   and the authority of his Christ.
> For the accuser of our brothers and sisters
>   has been thrown down to earth—
> the one who accuses them
>   before our God day and night.
> —REVELATION 12:10

How was Satan defeated? John explains that it took two weapons:

And they have defeated him by the blood of the
   Lamb
  and by their testimony.
And they did not love their lives so much
  that they were afraid to die.

—REVELATION 12:11

We don't usually think of Jesus's blood as a weapon, but it has the power to conquer sin, death, and Satan. A pastor in the state of Washington was driving on a country road one day when a flock of sheep crossed in front of him. As he waited, he met the shepherd. For many years the pastor had taught his congregation about the power of Jesus's blood, but he saw an opportunity to learn a practical lesson from an expert. He asked the shepherd, "Would you please tell me what 'the blood of the lamb' means?"

The shepherd smiled as he began his explanation. "During lambing season both the lambs and their mothers, the ewes, are very vulnerable—to wolves, wild dogs, cold, and diseases. Sometimes several lambs die, leaving their mothers with plenty of milk. At the same time some ewes die, leaving their lambs as orphans. If these orphans don't get milk, they'll die too. The ewes without lambs, though, won't nurse the orphans. They'll only feed their own. When this happens, I find a ewe's dead lamb, cut its throat, and pour its blood on one of the orphans. The ewe smells the blood of her baby and adopts the orphan as her own. When the orphan is covered with the blood of the lamb, it's accepted, it thrives, and it grows. Actually, it's the lamb's only chance to live."

The pastor instantly made the connection: When we're covered with the Lamb's blood, we're accepted so we can receive nourishment and grow. Without the Lamb's blood we surely die. In Colossians Paul explained that the blood of Jesus forgives all our sins, and his blood was so powerful it "disarmed the spiritual rulers and authorities. He shamed them publicly by his victory over them on the cross" (Col. 2:15). We never have to feel defeated. We're never powerless and hopeless. The blood of Jesus is a powerful weapon against the accusations, plots, and devices of the enemy.

Satan has words and lies, but his power is limited. In fact, his power was defeated at the cross of Jesus. The blood of Christ is powerful to bring down strongholds, overcome demonic forces, and challenge lies spoken against us. In the celestial courtroom Jesus has already paid our debt with the most precious, costly commodity in the universe: His own blood.

The second weapon John describes is the testimony of believers. Our witness of faith isn't some soft, happy, self-fulfillment slogan. John said our ultimate testimony is our willingness to die for Jesus. Today many of us cower when people look at us sideways when we tell them about Jesus. Actually, very few of us encounter genuine opposition when we share our faith. In the time John wrote Revelation, things were different. Christians were dying because they stood up and spoke out about Jesus Christ. Some were thrown to lions in the coliseum, bulls gored some, a few were covered with pitch and set on fire to light the emperor's terrace, and some died when molten lead was poured into holes bored in their skulls.[2] Looking sideways at them? Not a problem. These people were willing to suffer and die because they were convinced Jesus was worth it.

Is Jesus worth it to you?

What's your testimony? Some of us think that our stories are lame because we weren't drug addicts or prostitutes or in gangs before Christ rescued us. We hear the dramatic stories, and we feel inferior. Here's the truth: Every story of being rescued from hell is dramatic. Every testimony of a life transformed is thrilling. Every saga of being delivered from the kingdom of darkness into the kingdom of God matters. And every story connects with someone who's listening. Never feel ashamed because you grew up in a home where your parents loved you. You were lost, in need of God's amazing grace! Tell people your story, and let God work in their hearts. He will. You can count on it.

TIME IS SHORT

When God pulled back the curtains for John, John saw the two weapons used by God's people, and he witnessed the intense conflict between Satan and the children of God. He wrote:

> Therefore, rejoice, O heavens!
>   And you who live in the heavens, rejoice!
> But terror will come on the earth and the sea,

for the devil has come down to you in great
anger,
knowing that he has little time.
—REVELATION 12:12

Today many people in churches focus almost
entirely on their own desires, their own hopes, their
own dreams, and their own needs—and they aren't
even aware of the violent war for people's souls going
on around them. As Jesus explained to the two audiences sitting and standing around Him, the angels in
heaven rejoice when anyone repents and finds Christ.
But Satan unleashes terror "in great anger." He uses
deception, temptation, and accusation to lull people
to sleep so they aren't alarmed by their sin. He has
done a masterful job convincing people they don't need
God at all and that grace is unnecessary. And if he
can't cause people to be complacent, he ruins their lives
with drugs, illicit sex, greed, jealousy, bitterness, pornography, and other enticements. All of these things
taste great at first, but they're poison to the heart, mind,
soul, body, and relationships.

Do you wonder if the devil is alive and active? Just
look around at two evidences: spiritual apathy and personal destruction. Everywhere you look, people don't
care about God, and they're destroying their lives with
things that promise to give them ultimate satisfaction
but can't deliver.

Time is short for us to get the word out. We have
more resources today than ever before in history. We
have books, magazines, the Internet, cell phones, and

global air travel to take the message of God's grace to our neighbor next door and to people on the other side of the planet. We can't change hearts on our own. God is the source, the channel, the power, and the authority. We have to pray—and pray like we mean it. God changes hearts as we pray. We can't afford to sit around and wonder who is going to reach out to addicts, gang members, and prostitutes—or our families and friends. We can't keep twiddling our thumbs while millions of women are captured and made sex slaves. We can't keep watching families be torn apart. Time is short. We need to get up and get going…now!

Pastor Larry Osborne said, "Life is too short and hell is too hot to just play church."[3]

OUT OF THE CLOSET

People who go to church but aren't excited enough to tell other people about Jesus need to do some self-examination. They need to ask, "Am I a Christian at all? If I am, what weeds of greed and worry are choking out the life of Christ in me? Am I thrilled to know Jesus, or am I secretly ashamed of Him?"

In some circles coming out of the closet is popular these days. Some Christians need to come out of the closet too.

No one is beyond the power of God's grace. It can change the hardest heart and the most apathetic attitude. Paul wrote:

Don't fool yourselves. Those who indulge in sexual sin, or who worship idols, or commit adultery, or are male prostitutes, or practice homosexuality, or are thieves, or greedy people, or drunkards, or are abusive, or cheat people— none of these will inherit the Kingdom of God. Some of you were once like that. But you were cleansed; you were made holy; you were made right with God by calling on the name of the Lord Jesus Christ and by the Spirit of our God
—1 CORINTHIANS 6:9–11

No matter who you are, no matter what you've done, no matter how far you have to go, God makes you right with Him as you call on the blood of Jesus.

TWO DESTINATIONS

In the first chapter we began our examination of Christianity Lite by looking at Jesus's contrast of two roads. Let's return there. In His most famous sermon Jesus warned, "You can enter God's Kingdom only through the narrow gate. The highway to hell is broad, and its gate is wide for the many who choose that way. But the gateway to life is very narrow and the road is difficult, and only a few ever find it" (Matt. 7:13–14).

- The two roads go in two different directions, and they have two different destinations. Every person has a choice. We can't ride two horses going in opposite directions. We have to pick one. The broad

road looks very appealing. People can do anything, believe anything, and pursue anything. Absolutely anything goes! Our flesh loves wide-open options; it doesn't like submission to a higher authority.

On the broad road travelers have lots of company. There's no shortage of people whose choices follow a hamburger chain's ad: "Have it your way!" They find plenty of people who affirm them in their sin and applaud them for stepping on people to get to the top. They compete with each other to see who can get away with the most foolishness and win the most toys. It seems like such fun...for a while. Eventually the broad road takes people to a certain destination: hell. It's a place of utter desolation—no friends, no joy, no light, no chances. In fact, it's where people experience the full measure and the logical consequences of their choices in this life. Nobody is standing on the top step of hell beating on the door and screaming to get out. It's where they wanted to go all along.

We have plenty of "broad road churches" preaching Christianity Lite. They accept everyone just the way they are, and they have no expectations of repentance, obedience, or sacrifice for those who attend. These pastors assure people they're "all going to heaven because there really is no hell."

Those who are on the narrow road are courageous and noble. I have the greatest respect for people who have—not perfectly but consistently—made the hard choices to follow Jesus in good times and bad. They are the heroes of the faith in our modern times. But those of us on the narrow road need to be careful. From our perspective the broad road often looks very appealing. In fact, many people on the narrow road envy those who are on the broad road. We look at their power, their money, their lavish lifestyles, their beauty, and their prestige, and we long to be just like them. The broad road is the source of unspeakable crimes and abuses, but more often it's subtle: It lures people in with seductive charms. It promises ease, plenty, and power with no cost to them and no sacrifice for others. No wonder it's so attractive! But it's a dead-end street.

On the broad road people quit when times are tough, and they blame everyone else (including God) for their troubles. They quit on their marriages, their kids, their work, and their friends. People on the narrow road have a different perspective about difficulties. They know they need God's sharpening, and every trial is God's file to shave off a little more selfishness and shape them with faith, hope, and love. God's curriculum of sufferings seems absurd to those on the broad road, but those on the narrow path realize it's essential for God to transform them so they become more useful in caring for others.

The apostle Paul was tough as nails, but in his last letter to the Corinthians we find an uncharacteristic emotion: he was afraid. What caused his fear? He told them, "But I fear that somehow your pure and undivided devotion to Christ will be corrupted, just as Eve was deceived by the cunning ways of the serpent"

(2 Cor. 11:3). He was afraid the Corinthians believed the lies of the enemy and were drifting down the broad road.

We have two huge choices in life. We have to decide which road we're going to travel. Then, if we choose the narrow road, we need to warn as many people as possible of the broad road's destructive consequences and invite them to follow Jesus and us on the narrow path.

Two roads, two destinations, two outcomes. What do we see when we walk past people each day? In his message "The Weight of Glory," C. S. Lewis encourages us to see people with an eye toward their eternal destiny. Someday we'll all arrive at our forever destination. We'll be changed—for better or worse. Lewis explains:

> It is a serious thing to live in a society of possible gods and goddesses, to remember that the dullest and most uninteresting person you talk to may one day be a creature which, if you saw it now, you would be strongly tempted to worship, or else a horror and a corruption such as you now meet, if at all, only in a nightmare. All day long we are, in some degree, helping each other to one or other of these destinations. It is in the light of these overwhelming possibilities, it is with the awe and the circumspection proper to them, that we should conduct all our dealings with one another, all friendships, all loves, all play, all politics. There are no *ordinary*

people. You have never talked to a mere mortal. Nations, cultures, arts, civilization—these are mortal, and their life is to ours as the life of a gnat. But it is immortals whom we joke with, work with, marry, snub, and exploit—immortal horrors or everlasting splendors.[4]

When we see people through the lenses of eternity, we become passionate about rescuing them! We realize incredible glory or everlasting shame awaits every person. Then the gospel of Christ is no longer just a nice story; it becomes our heart's cry and the reason we live. We no longer are afraid of what people think of us; we'll do anything to assure them of God's magnificent grace, love, and power.

Most of the people you see every day are on the broad road. What do you see when you look at them? Do you see them as "immortal horrors or everlasting splendors," or do you see only their hair, clothes, jewelry, titles, and other things that don't matter at all?

Wake up! Understand what Jesus was saying. Get on the right road, and invite everyone you see to join you.

NEVER TOO LATE

I met a man who was an unlikely candidate for the grace of God. Doug is six feet, five inches tall and weighs 255 pounds—concrete with arms. He's a black belt, super heavyweight champion in karate. When he was younger, he hung out with a rough crowd, and eventually he joined Hell's Angels. When the movie came out about the group years ago, one of the characters portrayed Doug. He wasn't just tough; he was the motorcycle gang's enforcer. He shot five people. He was the meanest, roughest guy around.

Doug's mother was a tiny woman with a huge heart. She was worried about her son, and she poured out her concerns to the Lord. One day Doug was hiding from the law at his mother's house. He was drunk and watching television to kill time. His mother went into the room, grabbed his big arms, looked into his face, and began speaking in tongues. Doug wanted to throw his mother through the window, but God gave him a vivid vision.

> When we see people through the lenses of eternity, we become passionate about rescuing them!

In his vision he saw a man carrying a cross. Another man stood over him beating him mercilessly with a whip. Over and over again the whip ripped the man's back. Doug remembered, "When I saw that scene, I thought, 'That's not a fair fight. Give the man time to get up so he can fight!'"

Doug yelled at the man with the whip, "You're such a chicken. If I ever find you, I'm going to kill you!"

In the vision the man with the whip nailed the other man to a cross. When he turned around, Doug was shocked. He related, "The man with the whip—the man who nailed the other to the cross—had my face. It was me!"

As his mother prayed, Doug's heart was shattered. He wept bitter but cleansing tears. He realized the man he had nailed to the cross wasn't going to fight him. It was Jesus, and He died for him. At that moment Doug was gloriously saved.

We can always find reasons to remain quiet. You may say, "Pastor Glen, you don't understand. I work around a lot of people who aren't saved. They're pretty rough." Or you may comment, "Pastor, my friends at school laugh at Christians. It's hard for me." Or, "All my friends drink. If I don't join them, they'll think I'm weird." There are dozens of excuses, and I've heard them all.

If you're around a lot of unbelievers, that's exactly where God wants you. We can't lead people to Jesus if we don't hang out with them, get to know them, and share life with them. We don't join them in their sin, but we love them in spite of their sins. Only the self-righteous, superior, holier-than-you crowd felt uncomfortable with Jesus. The sinners sensed His love, and they flocked to Him. What does it mean to "be like Jesus"? It may mean many things, but surely one of them is being a true friend to sinners.

Scottish missionary and Arabic scholar John Keith Falconer commented, "I have but one candle of life to burn, and I would rather burn it out in a land filled with darkness than in a land flooded with light."

And in *How to Give Away Your Faith* Paul Little wrote, "The Holy Spirit can't save saints or seats. If we don't know any non-Christians, how can we introduce them to the Savior?"[5]

Someday we'll stand before Jesus to give an account

of our lives since the day we trusted in Him. Every attitude, motive, and action will pass through the fire at the judgment seat of Christ. All of our choices that were selfish or apathetic will burn up. Only those things done for Christ's honor will last into the new heaven and new earth. Don't be surprised on that day.

Christianity Lite entertains us, but it doesn't nourish and excite us. It starts well but is a poor finisher.

You can *do* better than that. You can *be* better than that. You can *trust* more deeply than that.

Don't be ashamed of the gospel. Be thrilled with Jesus—so thrilled that you can't stop talking about Him.

CONSIDER THIS...

1. Have you ever lost something really important? How did you respond when you realized it was lost? If you found it, how did you feel then?

2. Why do you think the angels party in heaven when someone trusts in Jesus? How do you think the two groups (outcasts and Pharisees) responded to Jesus's stories of the lost sheep, the lost coin, and the lost son? If unbelievers are "reading your life," what do they perceive about Jesus, the Christian life, hope, love, and purpose? Are you happy with the book of your life? Why or why not?

3. In what way is Jesus's blood a weapon? How do we use it?

4. How is our testimony a weapon? How can we sharpen it?

5. In what way is time short for us? How does this fact motivate you?

6. In Christianity Lite in what way are people "saved without sharing"? Why aren't they excited about Jesus? Why aren't they willing to give up their lives for Jesus's sake?

7. What's the most powerful motivation for you to tell people about Jesus?

8. Who are some people God is putting on your heart?

eight

CHOSEN TO CHANGE THE WORLD

*If Christ lives in us, controlling our personalities, we
will leave glorious marks on the lives we touch. Not
because of our lovely characters, but because of his.*[1]
—EUGENIA PRICE

C HRIST ALWAYS HAS higher purposes and bigger
plans than we can imagine—and all of us are
invited to join Him. God has crafted every
believer to accomplish a specific, individual mission.
Paul reminded us: "For we are God's masterpiece. He
has created us anew in Christ Jesus, so we can do the
good things he planned for us long ago" (Eph. 2:10).

MASTERPIECE

God's masterpiece? You? Me? Are we kidding ourselves?

Yes, the Creator of the universe used His incredible
skill and wisdom in shaping each of us—always with
a divine purpose of expanding His kingdom on earth.
Nothing less than that!

In Christianity Lite people aren't interested in "doing good things" for God because they're completely focused on acquiring pleasure, fame, and possessions. Some people who genuinely love God, though, feel disconnected from God's purposes for a very different reason. They believe they're disqualified because of shameful past sins or devastating past wounds. They look at their lives and see only fragments of broken dreams. They wish they could go back and make better decisions or avoid being hurt, but that's not possible. They feel hopeless and discouraged. God's magnificent purposes may be for others, they've concluded, but not for them.

They need to remember a crucial fact: the powerful grace of God rules over the past, the present, and the future. Moses was a murderer who fled for his life and lived on the backside of nowhere for forty years, but God hadn't forgotten him. He used Moses to confront the most powerful ruler in the world and lead God's people out of slavery. Joseph had big dreams as a kid, but God took him on a detour through betrayal, slavery, and imprisonment before he emerged to save Egypt and his family from famine. Peter denied (to a little girl!) that he even knew Jesus, but the Lord restored the fisherman and used him to launch the church. Paul was involved in kidnapping and murder before Jesus appeared to him on the road to Damascus and turned his life around. And when I was in college, I was more interested in the Mardi Gras than God until I met Christ.

Every Christian is a masterpiece of God's mercy, created and crafted for great things. We only need to make ourselves available to Him. God has chosen all of us to change the world.

God never wastes our past or our pain. He masterfully weaves even the darkest strands of our lives into the fabric of His good purposes. He uses our deepest sins to help us appreciate His grace, and He uses our wounds to give us compassion for others who suffer. Every person has a unique story, and every story is powerful. Everyone, though, has the power to say no to God's invitation and summons.

CALLED AND CHOSEN

Not long before His crucifixion Jesus told a story of a king sending his servants to invite people to come to his son's wedding feast. It was going to be an elaborate celebration, but those who were invited refused to come. The king was angry. Their refusal wasn't just a dumb, selfish choice; they insulted their king! In response he sent his servants out into the streets and farms to invite anyone who would come. Soon the banquet hall was filled, but there was a problem. Some of the people who showed up weren't dressed in wedding clothes. Jesus's point was that some people who come to church aren't "wearing" the grace of God, and Christ's love and power haven't transformed their hearts. Jesus concluded the story with a powerful observation: "For many are called, but few are chosen" (Matt. 22:14).

The gospel is available to every person in every corner

of the globe, but only a few truly embrace it. In the story the king chose those he invited, but they also had a choice: to attend or not—and if they attended, they could choose to wear wedding clothes of grace or dress in self-righteous rags.

God often uses us from the first day we trust in Jesus, but He takes us through a training program to prepare us for even more. To use a different metaphor, those who are chosen by God and who choose God above all else—who count the cost and are willing to pay the price— are like tempered steel. A metalsmith making a fine sword repeatedly heats the steel and folds it. Each time the metal gets a little stronger. When we come into God's family, He doesn't leave us alone. He is a master craftsman who puts us in the heat of difficulties and folds us with troubles. If we stay in His hands, we become strong, tempered steel— and He can use us as sharp instruments to have an impact on everyone around us. He prepares us to do our part to change the world.

God never wastes our past or our pain.

Some people have the marks of leadership before they come to Christ. Years ago I spoke at a high school, and I noticed a young man obviously admired by others in his class. Wherever he went, others followed. After my message he came up and introduced himself and asked, "Do you ever counsel young people?"

I answered, "Call and make an appointment. I'd be glad to meet with you."

Two weeks later this young man came to my office. He explained, "I don't know if you can help me. It doesn't seem like anybody can. I have dreams...horrible dreams."

He told me that about four nights every week he dreamed that he was killed in terrible, tragic ways. He described several of these dreams to me, and I asked, "What kind of music do you listen to?"

He looked a little surprised at my question, and then he answered, "I like death metal."

I wondered why he hadn't connected the dots. The dots and lines seemed pretty clear to me. I explained, "What goes into our ears shapes our minds and our dreams." This young man brought a sketchbook to our meeting. As we talked, he showed it to me. He was a very talented artist. He had page after page of beautifully rendered drawings of album covers—of the death metal bands. One of his drawings caught my eye. It was a young man with hollow eyes and a dead expression on his face.

I asked, "Bryan, is that you?" He nodded. I looked more closely at the artwork. It was crafted entirely from the repetition of two letters: m-e. He had become totally absorbed in his own hurts, fears, anger, and insecurities. From the outside this young man seemed to have it all together, but he was dying inside. I assured him, "Bryan, if you'll give your life to the Lord, He'll transform your mind, your heart, *and* your dreams."

He squirmed in his chair. It wasn't the answer he wanted to hear. I asked a few more questions, and he told me he was going to be eighteen in a few months. I knew what that meant. He was going to be legal. He could go into bars, clubs, and all kinds of places. He didn't want to miss out on any of that!

I talked to Bryan about the hope and forgiveness Christ offers. I said, "God has given you special talents and an unusual ability to lead people. God wants to use you to change the world. Will you follow Him?"

He smiled and shook his head. "I don't want to miss out on a good time," he explained.

I tried to talk to him about the consequences of his decision, but he didn't want to hear it. As he resisted, the Lord gave me a message for him. I haven't gotten this kind of word from God about someone before or since, but He gave me a glimpse into Bryan's future. I told him flatly, "Bryan, if you don't turn your life over to Jesus, in six months you will be the victim of an assault. In a year you'll have a sexually transmitted disease, and in eighteen months you'll be strung out on drugs and living with an addict. You can change all this by trusting in Jesus."

Bryan looked surprised at my prophetic words, but he smiled dismissively and said, "Thanks for telling me, but I'll take my chances." He walked out.

Six months later my phone rang. It was Bryan. He said, "Pastor, you were right. Last night I was assaulted after leaving a bar."

I responded, "I'm so sorry. Bryan, it's not too late. God has chosen you to change the world. Will you turn your life over to Him?"

"No," he replied. "I'm not ready for that. There's too much fun out here."

Another half a year passed, and Bryan called again. He said, "Pastor, I'm at the doctor's office being treated for an STD."

"I'm so sorry to hear about that," I told him. "Are you ready now to turn to Jesus? He'll forgive, He'll heal, and He'll give you a future."

"Thanks, Pastor Glen," he said as he blew me off. "I'm not interested."

I asked him, "Why are you calling me?"

He said, "Because you have always told me the truth, but I'm still not ready."

About six months later my phone rang. It was Bryan. He explained, "Pastor Glen, you were right again. I'm taking pills, drinking, and smoking crack. And I'm living with a dealer."

"Why are you calling, Bryan?" I asked him. "Are you ready to give your heart to Jesus? Are you ready to join Him in changing the world?"

"No, pastor," he said softly with profound sadness. "No, it's just not me."

I haven't heard from him since that day. He was chosen to change the world, but he said no.

Years ago I met another high school student when I was establishing a Christian club at a school. This kid's name was Stephanie. She was a born leader, but she was taking people in the wrong direction. Stephanie was a bully: big, brash, and loud. When she saw me in the hall, she announced, "Hey, are you the preacher who's trying to start a club *at my school?*"

"Yes, I am." I spoke loudly enough so everyone could hear me.

She confronted me as she looked around and shouted, "Well, I'm starting an atheist club."

I answered her challenge. "I can see you're a big deal in the school hall, but I dare you to come to one of my meetings. Come on, Ms. Atheist, and see if you can handle it. Are you woman enough?"

She almost growled. "I'll be there."

I told her, "I'll believe it when I see it."

A few days later Stephanie showed up at my meeting and sat on the front row. She crossed her arms and scowled. Her posture showed she was defying me. As I spoke, however, her mood softened. When my talk was over, she came up to me and said, "Hey, that was pretty good."

As we talked, I could tell God was knocking on the door of her heart, but she kept it locked tight. I asked, "Stephanie, God has chosen you to change the world. Are you ready to put yourself in His hands?"

She almost laughed. "No way, pastor. No way." Stephanie walked out, and I seldom saw her again. She was chosen to change the world, but she said no.

A few years ago I met a gifted athlete who had potential to play in the NFL. James had it all: size, speed, quickness, and an innate sense of the game. I saw terrific leadership abilities in him, and I told him God had chosen him to change the world—first the football team, and who knows after that. But James was also filled with anger and insecurity. His stepfather had beaten him mercilessly and repeatedly when he was a boy, and he carried a load of rage. Anger was his constant companion, and it sabotaged his life. He hated to be punished, but he invited the coaches' discipline by being late to practice or not following other rules. When they gave him consequences, he exploded and blamed them. To try to control him, the coaches increased the consequences: they benched James for the start of a big game. He got so angry that he walked off the sidelines during a game and never came back. He threw away his present and his future by letting his past dictate his life. He was chosen to change the world, but he said no.

The Bible shows us plenty of examples of people who misused their freedom to choose. A rich, young, respected man came to Jesus expecting to be affirmed in his self-absorbed behavior. He was religious, but only to prove to himself and others that he deserved God's blessings. Jesus had a different agenda. He told the man to sell everything he had, give it to the poor, and follow Him. The man counted the cost and said, "No thanks." As he walked away, both he and Jesus were saddened by his decision.

The twelve disciples had front row seats on the fulfillment of God's magnificent promises. For more than three years they watched Jesus heal the sick, restore sight to blind people, and raise the dead. They heard Him teach about the kingdom of God and refute the venomous attacks of the Pharisees. Jesus invited the twelve disciples to change the world, and He gave them the very best training anyone could ever receive. But one of them gave up the Lord of life for thirty silver coins. Today parents don't name their children "Judas."

When the chief priests and elders handed Jesus over to the Romans to be killed, Pilate had a different idea. It was his custom to release one prisoner at the Passover. He wanted to release Jesus, but the crowd insisted that he free Barabbas, a man who had plotted insurrection and committed murder. The Son of God gave Himself so Barabbas could go free. Ironically Barabbas's name means "the son of the father." So...the Son of the Father gave His life for "the son of the father." If anyone ever had a testimony of grace and liberation, it was this guy! God offered him a chance to proclaim His message and change the world, but we never hear from him again. Given the opportunity, Barabbas said no.

A BETTER CHOICE

God has a wonderful adventure for every person. Some people want none of it, but others who seemed hopelessly lost have said yes to Jesus. They've been chosen to change the world, and they've jumped in with both feet! They're young and old, rich and poor, and come from different ethnic backgrounds. When Christ captures our hearts, it doesn't matter who we are, what we've done, or where we're from. He's glad to use us.

Jane was a high school student who became a Christian when she was a freshman. When she was a senior, she realized she hadn't done much to tell people about Jesus. She asked me to pray for her. After we prayed, I told her I was sure God was going to use her in a big way before she graduated.

God gave her an idea. Her speech teacher assigned the class to give talks about an object...any object. When it was her turn, Jane stood in front of the class holding a paper bag. She explained, "The object I want to talk about is in this bag. A few years ago my life was going in the wrong direction. I had no hope and no future, but the object in this bag had the power to transform my life. It's the most powerful thing in the universe. It can free an addict from drugs, it can restore a broken relationship, and it can give hope to someone who is hopeless." Jane talked about how the item in her bag radically changed her life and gave her purpose, joy, and more love than she ever imagined possible.

After a few minutes students were on the edge of their seats. They wanted to know, "What's in the bag?"

Jane reached in and pulled out her Bible. She turned to the teacher and asked, "Mrs. Smith, would it be OK if I talk about the author of my book?"

It was a public school, so the teacher was a bit confused about the protocol of talking about spiritual matters in school. Finally she nodded, "Sure, go ahead."

Jane explained, "The author of my book transformed my life, changed my heart, and saved my soul. Because of Him I have peace beyond understanding. The author of this book is Jesus Christ, the Son of God."

She again turned to the teacher with a question:

"Can I ask if people want to accept the author of my book?"

The teacher smiled weakly and said, "Oh, I guess so."

Jane faced the class and explained, "If you want the love, forgiveness, and power Jesus offers, just raise your hand."

Fifteen students in the classroom raised their hands!

When I had asked Jane if she had been chosen to change the world, she emphatically said, "Yes!" And God used her.

When I met Robbie, he was into Goth. He wore black pants, black boots, black shirts, and I'm sure he had black underwear (though that's just a calculated guess). The only thing not black was his hair—it was bright red! He painted on black mascara to make himself look more sinister. I told him I was going to start a Bible club. He announced he was going to start a devil club. I responded, "Bring it on!"

He had terrific leadership talents. I told him, "Robbie, I know you're into the occult, but God has chosen you to change the world."

He just laughed.

Months later I started a meeting and glanced at the crowd. Everybody there looked normal—except for one person dressed in black. It was Robbie. As I finished the invitation, I saw something very strange. Robbie was at the altar, and black mascara was running down his face. I said, "Hey, it's good to see you tonight. I didn't think you'd come. I noticed your tears. What's going on in your heart?"

He looked at me with a slight smile and asked, "Do you really want to know?"

"Sure," I told him.

He looked down as he explained, "The devil told me that if I'd come tonight and kill you, he'd give me incredible power. I was here to murder you tonight."

I hadn't heard that one before. I caught my breath and asked, "So what happened?"

He looked into my eyes, "When I was getting ready to stand up to shoot you, some force pushed my chest back into the seat and locked my arms to the chair. I felt paralyzed. I couldn't move. When I looked up, I saw an angel behind you. It was about twenty feet tall. I realized at that moment that the devil had lied to me all these years. I thought he had power, but your God has all the power. I want to be saved. I want to follow Jesus."

When Robbie was asked to change the world, he said, "Yes!" He started a Christian organization, went to college, and published a newspaper honoring Jesus. Today he serves as a missionary overseas (undoubtedly without mascara).

I know people from every walk of life who have answered Jesus's challenge and are changing the world. Some are in youth ministry, some care for the poor and outcasts, and others are in businesses and homes. We don't have to be missionaries to be effective in God's kingdom. He'll use us wherever we are.

WAKE UP!

When we look around us, we see people going about their normal, everyday lives—just as they have since Jesus rose into heaven. On that day there was a sense of urgency, but no longer. Today our minds focus on all the things that promise to make us comfortable, happy, and successful. We compare our lives with the people on television or in the nicer neighborhoods, and we feel like we've gotten a raw deal. When our hearts are filled with earthly things, we don't long for the heavenly. We may go to church, give in the offering, and serve in different ways, but we're just going through the motions. We're spiritually asleep.

We're spiritually asleep when 10 percent of Americans suffer from depression each year.[2]

We're spiritually asleep when we march against polluting our planet with toxins but no one seems to care that we're polluting our minds with pornography.

We're spiritually asleep when our country spends about $60 billion every year on alcohol to numb our pain.[3]

We're spiritually asleep when a serial killer has more rights in our courts than the Ten Commandments.

We're asleep when abortion is considered a viable option for birth control.

We need to wake up!

It's time to stop playing games with church and God. There's too much at stake. Near the end of his letter to the Romans, Paul urged them, "This is all the more urgent, for you know how late it is; time is running out.

Wake up, for our salvation is nearer now than when we first believed. The night is almost gone; the day of salvation will soon be here. So remove your dark deeds like dirty clothes, and put on the shining armor of right living" (Rom. 13:11–12).

What would Paul say to the church today? What would he say to you and me?

If we listen carefully, we'll notice three different kinds of wake-up calls: silence, sorrow, and crises. God is trying to get our attention. Will we listen?

Silence

It's not enough for the church to have beautiful buildings and lovely music. We can't be satisfied with putting people in seats so we can pat ourselves on the back. The world is going to hell, and it's up to us to warn them, beg them, and lead them to the Savior. There is no Plan B. The need for salvation and healing has never been greater, but in many churches and countless hearts God seems to be distant, absent, and silent. We see plenty of religious activity but little evidence of God's awesome voice and power.

If we read the Bible, we'll see dramatic indications that God isn't only present; He's moving in dramatic ways! And if we really pay attention, we realize the culmination of all of history is right around the corner—the end is coming soon.

Are there clear signs the end is near? Jesus said to look for wars and rumors of wars. Every corner of the globe is experiencing armed conflict, and we live under constant threats from Iran, North Korea, and Islamist extremists. He said there will be famines. Every day about sixteen thousand children around the world die from starvation.[4] Millions of people are perishing from drought and hunger in Africa, and millions more suffer from severe malnutrition in many places on earth—even in America, where one in six is affected by hunger.[5] Jesus said there would be an increase in earthquakes. In recent years cataclysmic earth shifts have killed hundreds of thousands in Indonesia, Haiti, and Peru. The number and severity of quakes are growing.

The signs are global and personal. Paul wrote to Timothy to warn him that a deep and pervasive character flaw would characterize the last days: extreme selfishness. He wrote, "For people will love only themselves and their money. They will be boastful and proud, scoffing at God.... They will betray their friends, be reckless, be puffed up with pride, and love pleasure rather than God." Paul draws the conclusion: "They will act religious, but they will reject the power that could make them godly. Stay away from people like that!" (2 Tim. 3:2, 4–5). How does God respond to a self-absorbed society? He's deafeningly quiet, and He withdraws His presence. People have their values in the wrong places.

The presence of God is more important than possessions.

The presence of God is more vital than popularity.

The presence of God is more significant than personal power.

If God is silent in our lives, we need to take a long,

hard look at the condition of our hearts. Are we selfish or sold-out? Are our eyes focused on our desires, or do we long for God's purposes to succeed? We need champions like David, Esther, Gideon, Deborah, and Daniel who will cry out to God to save our land. We need people with a backbone like Shadrach, Meshach, and Abednego who will stand up for truth no matter what the cost.

> If God is silent in our lives, we need to take a long, hard look at the condition of our hearts.

We need people who will wake up and follow Christ. He is looking for people who will say, "Lord, take everything I have. Take my health. Take my reputation, but don't take Your presence from me!" Those are the kind of people He uses to change the world.

Sorrow

One of the sure signs we're awake to God is the realization of our sin and shame. Some pastors today do their best to keep their people from feeling bad about their sins. They preach a feel-good message, but that's only part of the gospel. The message of grace is that we're more evil than we ever imagined. Our hearts are dark, and our motives are selfish. When we stand in the brilliant light of God's holiness, we realize we're terribly unclean. We've betrayed God, ignored Him, and tried to use Him for our selfish purposes. These aren't things God winks at. They grieve Him. When we face the reality of our sin, we're stricken with sorrow—and then we're ready to be washed with the amazing grace of God. We can't appreciate the heights of His love until we're aware of the depths of our sin. We can't be grateful for the width of His forgiveness until we're aware of the breadth of our selfishness. Paradoxically sorrow is an essential ingredient in a life of faith, joy, love, and hope.

Paul called the Corinthians out about their sins. He pointed to their pride, favoritism, and sexual promiscuity, among others. He sent them a scathing letter to call them to repent. When he got word back they had read the letter and turned to Christ, he took the opportunity to describe two very different kinds of remorse. One points to Jesus; the other leads only to depression. He wrote:

> Now I am glad I sent it, not because it hurt you, but because the pain caused you to repent and change your ways. It was the kind of sorrow God wants his people to have, so you were not harmed by us in any way. For the kind of sorrow God wants us to experience leads us away from sin and results in salvation. There's no regret for that kind of sorrow. But worldly sorrow, which lacks repentance, results in spiritual death.
>
> —2 CORINTHIANS 7:9–10

If we had an operable cancer but a doctor offered only a painkiller, we'd rightly accuse him of malpractice. We'd walk out of his office and find a doctor who would do the painful surgery to rid us of the disease. It's no different with spiritual cancer. Many people go to churches where the pastor prescribes painkillers instead of exposing ugly, deadly sin. Spiritual sedatives feel good for the moment, but having the courage to be honest is the only way sin can be eradicated. Forgiveness requires truth about two things: the depravity in our hearts and the cleansing blood of Jesus.

If your church only prescribes painkillers, leave it. Find one where the pastor is honest about the reality of sin. That's the only way to experience Christ's healing, forgiving power.

If you feel deep sorrow over your sin, that's a really good sign you're alive to God. If gossip is a game, if lying is fun, if pornography is a pleasure, and if other sins are no big deal, you have big problems. You're not just asleep—you're dead.

You need God to wake you up and give you new life so you can be like Lazarus and come out of the tomb in your grave clothes!

Some people respond, "Well, pastor, I don't want to feel bad. That doesn't seem right. Surely pain isn't in God's plan, is it?"

This brings us back to a point I made in the first chapter: Jesus didn't come to hurt us; He came to kill us. If we want to follow Him, we must deny ourselves, crucify the flesh, die to our flesh and selfish desires, and let the Spirit of God live through us. That's what it means to die to self and live to God. Anything less may taste great, but it can't fill the gnawing emptiness in our hearts. We were made for more than painkillers and empty pleasures. We were meant to live an adventure, but first we have to die.

Crises

If we think faith in God guarantees a hassle-free life, we need to think again. Jesus promised blessings, but with persecution. He promised peace in times of trouble. He assured us that our obedience is a demonstration that we're all-in with God, which invites the master gardener to prune us so we'll bear more fruit. In other words, a life of faith necessarily involves difficulties. There's no getting around this fact.

Crises accomplish two important things: they scrape away all the fluff in our lives and reveal the true contents of our hearts, and they drive us deeper into the heart of God in radical dependence. Times of trouble are a watershed—we either run *to* God or *away from* Him. God wants to use every event in our lives to shape us. In *Reaching for the Invisible God* Philip Yancey explains, "Gregory of Nicea once called St. Basil's faith 'ambidextrous' because he welcomed pleasures with the right hand and afflictions with the left, convinced both would serve God's design for him."[6] When we trust God's sovereignty, purposes, and goodness in the middle of our suffering, we trust Him to teach us life's most important lessons. As we learn, we become humbler, stronger, and wiser. We realize the value of suffering in our spiritual growth. Gradually we care more about God and His kingdom than our petty desires. We want to change the world instead of blending into it.

Are you preparing your heart for the inevitable crises you're going to face? Or are you a dad who has abdicated spiritual leadership of your family to your wife? Are you a mom who blames her no-good husband for not being the man he should be and lives in bitterness and self-pity? Are you a kid who finds all kinds of excuses for walking away from God and pursuing excitement and pleasure? Get ready—a crisis is coming. If it comes and you want to run from God, be honest, admit it, and be brave enough to cling to Him in spite of your feelings. Your family is counting on your courage. Don't let them down.

Crises come in all shapes and sizes, but one thing is always true: we didn't expect them. It may be a lost job, a car wreck, a prodigal child, bankruptcy, betrayal by a spouse, or the dreaded word from the doctor that the tests showed the tumor is malignant. In hospitals, living rooms, and my office I've seen how a crisis surfaces a person's true character and exposes actual beliefs about God. Years ago my sister Linda was diagnosed with cancer. Together we asked God for the miracle of healing. For months she battled the disease. As her condition deteriorated, she never stopped depending on God. In the last days of the disease, her faith was stronger than ever, and she poured out her love for her children. She was never bitter. She never was disappointed in God. She was healed when she passed into God's presence. Her faith was gloriously vindicated.

I want to be like Linda. I want to hold tightly to God whether I'm healthy or if I'm sick, if I'm rich or poor, if things go well or the bottom drops out.

READY OR NOT?

Have you answered God's call to change the world? Are you awake, or are you still asleep? Are you paying attention to God's silence, your sorrow over sin, and the crises you face? It's your call. God is waiting, but He may not wait long.

> We want to change the world instead of blending into it.

Just before Jesus was arrested and crucified on the cross, He told a number of parables about the importance of being ready. One story was about ten virgins who were bridesmaids at a wedding. They had an assignment: they were to light lamps at night to show the way for the groom to come to his beautiful bride. At midnight the call came: "Look, the bridegroom is coming! Come out and meet him!"

Five of the virgins were ready. They had put oil in their lamps, and they lit the path for the groom. The other five, though, hadn't prepared for the event. At the last minute they scurried around to find some oil, but they missed their chance. They were too late. When they finally got back, they banged on the door. The groom replied, "Believe me, I don't know you!"

Jesus made sure His audience got the point. He explained, "So you, too, must keep watch! For you do not know the day or hour of my return" (Matt. 25:13).

The Christian life isn't a game, and it's not a spa. The kingdom of God is the most important reality in the universe. Jesus, the Bridegroom, is coming back soon. We don't know the exact date, but we need to be ready. We can keep fiddling around and waste our lives on frivolity, or we can invest it in honoring the One who is our greatest treasure. Jesus Christ is worthy of our life and our death. When we have even a hint of His greatness and grace, we'll pay any price to know Him, follow Him, and live for Him.

We need more than a diluted, decaffeinated version of discipleship. We need the real thing.

We'll even be willing to die.

CONSIDER THIS...

1. Read Ephesians 2:10. In what way are you God's masterpiece? Do you see yourself that way? If not, what difference would it make if you did?

2. Has God chosen you to change the world? How do you know? How have you responded so far?

3. What are some reasons people say no to God's invitation to change the world? What are some reasons they say yes?

4. What are some signs people are spiritually asleep? Which of these seem most alarming to you?

5. Describe how God's silence, sorrow, and crises can be wake-up calls for us. Which of these have you heard recently? Did you run from God or to Him? Describe your response. Do you need to make any adjustments?

6. Read Matthew 25:1–13. Are you ready for Jesus's return? Why or why not?

7. What is the most important thing you've learned from this book? How are you applying it? How do you need to apply it better?

8. Whom do you know who needs to read this book and become a real disciple?

Appendix

USING *CHRISTIANITY LITE* IN CLASSES AND GROUPS

THIS BOOK IS designed for individual study, small groups, and classes. The best way to absorb and apply these principles is for each person to individually study and answer the questions at the end of each chapter and then to discuss them in either a class or a group environment.

Each chapter's questions are designed to promote reflection, application, and discussion. Order enough copies of the book for everyone to have a copy. For couples, encourage both to have their own book so they can record their individual reflections.

A recommended schedule for a small group or class might be:

- Week 1: Introduce the material. As a group leader tell your story, share your hopes for the group, and provide books for each person. Encourage people to read the assigned chapter each week and answer the questions.

- Weeks 2–9: Each week introduce the topic for the week and share a story of how God has used the principles in your life. In small groups, lead people through a discussion of the questions at the end of the chapter. In classes, teach the principles in each chapter, use personal illustrations, and invite discussion.

PERSONALIZE EACH LESSON

Don't feel pressured to cover every question in your group discussions. Pick out three or four that had the biggest impact on you and focus on those, or ask people in the group to share their responses to the questions that meant the most to them that week.

Make sure you personalize the principles and applications. At least once in each group meeting add your own story to illustrate a particular point.

Make the Scriptures come alive. Far too often we read the Bible like it's a phone book, with little or no emotion. Paint a vivid picture for people. Provide insights about the context of people's encounters with God, and help people in your class or group sense the emotions of specific people in each scene.

FOCUS ON APPLICATION

The questions at the end of each chapter and your encouragement to group members to be authentic will help your group take big steps to apply the principles they're learning. Share how you are applying the principles in particular chapters each week, and encourage them to take steps of growth too.

THREE TYPES OF QUESTIONS

If you have led groups for a few years, you already understand the importance of using open questions to stimulate discussion. Three types of questions are *limiting*, *leading*, and *open*. Many of the questions at the end of each lesson are open questions.

Limiting questions focus on an obvious answer, such as, "What does Jesus call Himself in John 10:11?" These don't stimulate reflection or discussion. If you want to use questions like this, follow them with thought-provoking, open questions.

Leading questions require the listener to guess what the leader has in mind, such as, "Why did Jesus use the metaphor of a shepherd in John 10?" (He was probably alluding to a passage in Ezekiel, but many people don't know that.) The teacher who asks a leading question has a definite answer in mind. Instead of asking this kind of question, you should just teach the point and perhaps ask an open question about the point you have made.

Open questions usually don't have right or wrong answers. They stimulate thinking, and they are far less threatening because the person answering doesn't risk ridicule for being wrong. These questions often begin with "Why do you think…?" or "What are some reasons that…?" or "How would you have felt in that situation?"

PREPARATION

As you prepare to teach this material in a group or class, consider these steps:

1. Carefully and thoughtfully read the book. Make notes, highlight key sections, quotes, or stories, and complete the reflection section at the end of each chapter. This will familiarize you with the entire scope of the content.

2. As you prepare for each week's class or group, read the corresponding chapter again and make additional notes.

3. Tailor the amount of content to the time allotted. You won't have time to cover all the questions, so pick the ones that are most pertinent.

4. Add your own stories to personalize the message and add impact.

5. Before and during your preparation, ask God to give you wisdom, clarity, and power. Trust Him to use your group to change people's lives.

6. Most people will get far more out of the group if they read the chapter and complete the reflection each week. Order books before the group or class begins or after the first week.

NOTES

CHAPTER 1
MORE ME, LESS GOD

1. From the back cover of the album *Aqualung*, original release date 1971.
2. Barna.org, "Barna Examines Trends in 14 Religious Factors Over 20 Years (1991 to 2011)," July 26, 2011, http://www.barna.org/faith -spirituality/504-barna-examines-trends-in-14 -religious-factors-over-20-years-1991-to-2011 (accessed July 9, 2012).
3. Barna.org, "New Marriage and Divorce Statistics Released," March 31, 2008, http://www.barna.org/ barna-update/article/15-familykids/42-new -marriage-and-divorce-statistics-released (accessed July 9, 2012).
4. Barna.org, "Morality Continues to Decay," November 3, 2003, http://www.barna.org/barna -update/article/5-barna-update/129-morality -continues-to-decay (accessed July 9, 2012).
5. Dietrich Bonhoeffer, *The Cost of Discipleship* (New York: The MacMillan Company, 1963), 17.
6. Ibid., 44–45.
7. Lewis Smedes, *Shame and Grace* (New York: Zondervan/HarperCollins, 1993), 50–51.
8. A. W. Tozer, *The Pursuit of God* (Harrisburg, PA: Christian Publications, 1948), 46.

CHAPTER 2
SAVED WITHOUT POWER

1. *Talladega Nights: The Legend of Ricky Bobby*, dir. Adam McKay (Sony Pictures Home Entertainment, 2006), DVD.
2. A. W. Tozer, *The Fellowship of the Burning Heart* (n.p.: Bridge-Logos Publishers, 2006), 19.
3. Augustine, *Sermons* 191.1, as quoted in Andrew Knowles and Pachomios Penkett, *Augustine and His World* (Oxford, England: Lion Publishing, 2004), 130.

CHAPTER 3
SAVED WITHOUT PRAYER

1. As quoted in ChurchLeaderGazette.com, August 2, 2009, http://churchleadergazette.com/clg/2009/08/there-is-not-in-the.html (accessed July 10, 2012).
2. As quoted in J. Heyward Rogers, *Prayers and Promises of the Bible—Smart Guide* (Nashville: Thomas Nelson, 2007), chapter 1.
3. Richard Foster, *Celebration of Discipline* (San Francisco: HarperSanFrancisco, 1988), 15.
4. "Come, My Soul, Thy Suit Prepare" by John Newton. Public domain.

CHAPTER 4
SAVED WITHOUT COST

1. These four categories have been adapted from a message by R. C. Ryle called "The Cost," cited at www.gracegems.org/Ryle/h05.htm (accessed July 11, 2012).

2. "Before the Throne of God Above" by Charitie
Lees Smith Bancroft. Public domain.

CHAPTER 5
SAVED WITHOUT OFFENSE

1. As quoted in QuotationsBook.com, *Quotes About Adversity* (n.p.: n.d.), 7. Viewed at Google Books.
2. Larry Crabb, *Finding God* (Grand Rapids, MI: Zondervan, 1993), 18.
3. Christian Smith, "On 'Moralistic Therapeutic Deism' as a U.S. Teenagers' Actual, Tacit, De Facto Religious Faith," www.scribd.com/doc/7699752/Moralistic-Therapudic-Deism-by-Christian-Smith (accessed July 11, 2012).
4. Voltaire, *Notebooks* (c 1735–c.1750).
5. Lewis Smedes, *Forgive and Forget* (New York: HarperOne, 2007), x.

CHAPTER 6
SAVED WITHOUT SERVICE

1. *The Words of Martin Luther King, Jr.*, selected and with introduction by Coretta Scott King (New York: Newmarket Press, 2008), 17. Viewed at Google Books.
2. *Festival Letters*, quoted by Eusebius, *Ecclesiastical History* 7.22, 1965 ed.
3. Rodney Stark, *The Rise of Christianity* (New York: HarperOne, 1996), 7, 73–94.
4. Os Guinness, *The Call* (Dallas: Word Publishing, 1998), 42–43.

CHAPTER 7
SAVED WITHOUT SHARING

1. As quoted in David Jeremiah, *Grace Givers: Amazing Stories of Grace in Action* (Nashville: Thomas Nelson, 2008).
2. These and other persecutions are described in James Hasting, ed., *A Dictionary of the Bible*, vol. 3 (1898). Various reprints of the earlier edition are available online and through booksellers.
3. Larry Osborne, pastor of North Coast Church, Vista, California. Quote cited at EvangelismCoach .org, "Evangelism Quotes and Quotations," http:// www.evangelismcoach.org/2008/evangelism -quotes-and-quotations/ (accessed July 13, 2012).
4. C. S. Lewis, "The Weight of Glory," a sermon delivered in Oxford, England, June 8, 1942, http:// www.verber.com/mark/xian/weight-of-glory.pdf (accessed July 13, 2012).
5. Paul Little, *How to Give Away Your Faith* (Downers Grove, IL: IVP Books, 2008), 27.

CHAPTER 8
CHOSEN TO CHANGE THE WORLD

1. Eugenia Price, *Woman to Woman* (Grand Rapids, MI: Zondervan, 1959), 241.
2. Maureen Salamon, "People With Depression May Not Reveal Symptoms to Their Doctor," *USA Today*, September 13, 2011, http://www .usatoday.com/news/health/medical/health/ medical/mentalhealth/story/2011-09-13/People -with-depression-may-not-reveal-symptoms-to-their -doctor/50386274/1 (accessed July 13, 2012).

3. Emily Bryson York, "Liquor, Wine Continue to Take Share From Beer Sales," *Chicago Tribune*, January 31, 2012, http://articles.chicagotribune .com/2012-01-31/business/ct-biz-0131-liquor -export-20120131_1_liquor-sales-alcohol-sales -david-ozgo (accessed July 13, 2012).
4. Bread for the World, "Global Hunger," http:// www.bread.org/hunger/global/ (accessed July 13, 2012).
5. FeedingAmerica.org, "Hunger Facts," http:// feedingamerica.org/hunger-in-america/hunger -facts.aspx (accessed July 13, 2012).
6. Philip Yancey, *Reaching for the Invisible God* (Grand Rapids, MI: Zondervan, 2000), 69.

FREE NEWSLETTERS
TO HELP EMPOWER YOUR LIFE

Why subscribe today?

❏ **DELIVERED DIRECTLY TO YOU.** All you have to do is open your inbox and read.

❏ **EXCLUSIVE CONTENT.** We cover the news overlooked by the mainstream press.

❏ **STAY CURRENT.** Find the latest court rulings, revivals, and cultural trends.

❏ **UPDATE OTHERS.** Easy to forward to friends and family with the click of your mouse.

CHOOSE THE E-NEWSLETTER THAT INTERESTS YOU MOST:

- Christian news
- Daily devotionals
- Spiritual empowerment
- And much, much more

SIGN UP AT: **http://freenewsletters.charismamag.com**

8178